JESUS WAS AN EPISCOPALIAN

(And You Can Be One Too!)

A Newcomer's Guide to the Episcopal Church

Chris Yaw

ISBN 978-1-59518-000-1

BIG THANKS

Learning to write a book is a bit like learning to play the violin.

So I must first thank my closest neighbors, the good people of St. Thomas Episcopal Church in Battle Creek, Michigan who lived below, above and next door to me kindly refusing to bang on the pipes and stomp on the floor as I slowly honed my craft. Much of this material came from sermons, forums and newcomer's classes. Big thanks to all who participated, endured and were courageous enough to offer a few tips. Special thanks goes to Joy E. Rogers for her unfailing leadership, confidence, and commitment to social justice.

Unlike detective programs, the names mentioned herein have not been changed (perhaps for lack of innocence...). The lives and ministries of all who appear have profoundly touched me—thank you. Lois Phelps, Kathy Surprenant and Deacon Dale Bennett reviewed early drafts of this book. The most helpful critique was offered by Mark Busse whose organizational skills I value almost as much as our friendship. Ginny Baldwin provided some priceless editing, commentary and moral support. Thanks to mentors without whose insight and cheerleading this book may not have come to print: Fred Borsch, Nancy Fitzgerald, Carol Anderson, Wendell N. Gibbs, and Rob Johnston. Thanks to Linda Grenz, editor extraordinaire, and Leader Resources for taking a risk. Thanks to Julie Diehl for her painstaking layout and design work. Thanks to John and Andree at McArthur photography for photo assistance and Dave Gaston for the bottomless well of moral support—we've come a long way since the Kensington playground.

To supportive friends along the way; Chris Deighan, Tom Fanta, Meg Brossy, Jackie and Eric Strand, Eastern Deanery clergy in the Diocese of Western Michigan, Bryan Grantz and the CREDO team for helping me dream. To Jim and Nancy Yaw who would have bought any book with my name on it—even if it doesn't include recipes.

And most of all big thanks to my dearly beloved Natalie who listened, edited, and encouraged at every step. Your patience, clarity of thought and advice mean more than you will ever know. I love you forever. Finally, to everyone who purchased this book, know that the profits go toward the charities mentioned in the pages ahead.

However if this was a gift (or you stole it) feel free to pay it forward by making a donation to one of these charities—perhaps a sum equivalent to the price of a violin lesson.

TABLE OF CONTENTS

INTRODUCTION

Jesus was an Episcopalian.

OK, busted.

I admit this is a ridiculously audacious anachronism
that calls into question our very intelligence.
Please forgive me for any unintended provocation.
Please don't key my car.

After all, we all know Jesus was a Lutheran.

Or a Roman Catholic.

Or a Malakara Syrian Orthodox.

Or a Methodist. Or a Non-Denominational.

Or a Two-Seed-in-the-Spirit Predestinarian Baptist.

(Yes, they do exist, just Google it).

Or Jesus was whatever flavor of religion that best suits us—from
a 'good teacher' to the 'Son of God.' And we can take our pick
of thousands and thousands of opinions about Jesus and about
churches that have been established through two millennia.

So why suggest that, among all these options, Jesus, the Jew, was an
Episcopalian?

Well, he wasn't.

But he was very interested in doing the kind of work that Episcopalians are up to: healing, fixing, re-building, praying,
teaching, preaching, loving and making disciples out of a
new generation of people who are searching for God.

And I believe the Episcopal way of following Jesus is the best way there is to equip a new generation of North American Christians to be disciples.

Sure, there are other ways.

That's because we are all different.

Sure, the Episcopal way does not work for everyone.

But for a large number of North American Christians, the Episcopal Church offers an unparalleled approach to being Christian in an increasingly difficult environment.

Why?

It's because Episcopalians have an incredibly snappy little suitcase chock full of beliefs, practices and traditions that provide a uniquely attractive way of "doing church" in the new millennium.

Yes, that means this book is about "church"—which means you already may be putting it back on the shelf.

And who would blame you?

We all know the Christian Church has been responsible for some pretty hideous things. It has had its share of ugly persecutions.

It has known its share of controversy. The Church is responsible for the Crusades, the Inquisition and a curiously stable supply of very colorful charlatans (anybody watch cable TV?).

Jesus' first followers feuded over who would preach the Gospel and where it would be spread (Acts 15:36-40).

Steamy arguments over Christ's divinity split first century Jews and Christians. And in the 17th century Russian Orthodox "Old Believers" separated from Moscow largely because they insisted on making the sign of the cross with two fingers instead of three.

We all know the Church, like all human institutions, is hopelessly flawed.

We all know that it has gravely hurt and offended countless numbers of people, maybe even you.

So here's one option:

We can look at our egregious faults, declare them impossibly irredeemable and do away with the whole institution, the good and the bad.

And here's another:

We can consider the viewpoint of the One who created it. If there is a God, and I would propose there is, God sees the Church differently than we do.

Much differently.

The Bible says that the Lord sees the Church as the earthly representation of the virtues of heaven—Jesus called this vision 'the Kingdom of God' (his number one preaching topic).

God sees the Church, through the lives of each one of its members, as bearers of the love, peace and forgiveness that are at the heart of God's reconciling plan for the world. St. Paul wrote that through the Church, God's nature is made manifest. (Ephesians 3:10)

This is the Christian vision.

This is the Church's vision.

This is my own church's vision.

I am an Episcopal priest and this book is about my church.

But it's not just about who we Episcopalians are, it's also about who we are becoming. In the last few generations the Episcopal Church has been evolving from an insulated bastion of the affluent and exclusive to a rising and articulate voice for the poor and persecuted.

It is a voice of inclusion and compassionate love.

We Episcopalians entered this new millennium with a renewed sense of who we are and what God is calling us to do, and the pages that follow are a modest attempt to tell you about our journey.

I write this book as someone who owes an immense debt to the Episcopal Church for its steadfast perseverance in following Christ.

I write this book as an Episcopalian, not meaning to speak for every Episcopalian (as if they would let me).

And I write this book as someone who believes that God is endlessly at work. God is actively working to redeem our every fault and frailty—

turning insignificant shepherd boys into kings (David), fleeing murderers into great leaders (Moses), and beat up and battered communities of Jesus-followers into shiny new avenues of spiritual transformation and hope for the world.

May the words that follow further open our eyes to the active work of God in the many faces of Jesus that find expression in a joyful myriad of earthly incarnations.

It is in this way that we can say, yes, Jesus is a Lutheran.

Yes, Jesus is a Predestinarian Baptist.

And yes, Jesus is even an Episcopalian.

1. DO

"We need to get busy about healing the world.
That's what we've been called to do.
We need to stop focusing on our internal conflicts.
The mission of the church is the centerpiece."

The Most Rev. Katharine Jefferts Schori
Presiding Bishop of the Episcopal Church

Who Me?

Down the road from where I live is a Veteran's hospital—where men and woman from around the country come to get treated for all kinds of illnesses. Some have physical problems. Some have mental problems. Most come for inpatient care. A few people live there.

My friend Glenn, a Vietnam vet, lived there.

Like everyone I've ever met who's faced combat, the battles they fought are rarely left on the battlefield. This was the case with Glenn. He spent his life fighting the demons in his head and was unable to do much of anything else. He used to call me a lot—sometimes every day, sometimes more than once a day, depending on how much of his medication he'd taken or failed to take. Glenn would call with odd requests that were often time consuming and costly.

When it got to be too much I asked a new member of the church named Ann if she wouldn't mind visiting Glenn. "Who me?" she said, "But I haven't been trained to do that, I wouldn't know what to say or how to act!" However, soon it became clear that I wasn't the only one asking her to visit Glenn. God was tugging on Ann's heart.

Ann, a self-described 'Who me?' person, agreed to start visiting Glenn. Ann faithfully visited Glenn for more than a year before he died. She took him Bible verses, sat with him, and prayed with him.

Not long after she began, she called to thank me. She said she was getting more out of her visits with Glenn than she ever thought possible. And Glenn was getting a lot out of them as well—by then I knew—he still called me, though not as often.

Ann made Glenn's last year far better than he, or she, could've imagined. God used Ann, a 'Who me?' person, to touch a life as only she could.

The fact is, God uses 'Who me?' people all the time.

Open your Bible and read up on Abraham (the doubter), Jacob and Esau, (conniving rascals from a dysfunctional family), and John the Baptist (an ornery man with a very bizarre diet) and you will see that they all asked the same question, 'Who me?' They had the same doubts as Ann and you and me. We all wonder why on earth God would want to use us to help heal the world's hurts.

But God uses us all the time.

One of the most famous 'Who me?' persons I know of is the lead singer of the rock band U2—his name is Paul Hewson, but most people know him as Bono.

As you probably know, he is not your average rock star. After decades in the sex, drugs, and rock and roll business Bono has somehow managed to steer clear of these siren calls and answer another one instead.

Once he delivered the keynote address at the National Prayer Breakfast in Washington, D.C. This was his 'Who me?' opening line: "Thank you Mr. President. If you're wondering what I'm doing here, at a prayer breakfast, well, so am I. I'm certainly not here as a man of the cloth, unless that cloth is leather."[1]

Bono went on to preach to the Washington, D.C. power brokers a sermon that might have muzzled even Donald Trump. He lectured on their responsibility to lead with humility and mercy. He quoted the Jewish Torah, the Muslim Koran and the Christian New Testament. He spoke persuasively about America's obligation to care for the world's poor through debt relief, medical assistance and global leadership.

Who Me?

AG NCIA BRASIL

Famous not just for music but for his message, Bono, the lead singer for U2 constantly chal-lenges the Church, "Christ's example is being demeaned by the church if they ignore the new leprosy, which is AIDS (or malaria, or TB, or all other scourges of extreme poverty). The church is the sleeping giant here. If it wakes up to what's going on in the rest of the world, it has a role to play. If it doesn't, it will be irrelevant." As spokes-man for numerous poverty and AIDS organizations, Bono's spiritual journey includes membership in the Anglican Church of Ireland, cousin to the Episcopal Church.

The Millennium Development Goals (MDGs)

These are eight goals to be achieved by 2015 that respond to the world's main development challenges. The MDGs are drawn from the actions and targets contained in the Millennium Declaration that was adopted by 189 nations—and signed by 147 heads of state and governments during the UN Millennium Summit in September 2000.

The eight MDGs break down into 18 quantifiable targets that are measured by 48 indicators.

- Goal 1: Eradicate extreme poverty and hunger
- Goal 2: Achieve universal primary education
- Goal 3: Promote gender equality and empower women
- Goal 4: Reduce child mortality
- Goal 5: Improve maternal health
- Goal 6: Combat HIV/AIDS, malaria and other diseases
- Goal 7: Ensure environmental sustainability
- Goal 8: Develop a Global Partnership for Development

The Episcopal Church is one of many churches that have made the realization of the MDGs a priority. Find out more at www.globalgood.org.

Bono is as surprised as you or I would be at the call that has emerged in his life—to help rally a new generation around the issues of AIDS and poverty.

But God is not only working on Bono. God is working on you and me too. It's because God has work to do.

God has plenty of work for us to do.

Never before has there been so much opportunity for serious hunger, poverty and disease to be addressed and maybe even wiped out by you and me and a new generation of caring people. You and I are standing at an amazing crossroad in world history—finally we are able to feed, clothe and even heal the world's most desperately poor.

"Extreme poverty can be ended, not in the time of our grandchildren, but our time" is the clarion call coming from poverty expert Jeffrey Sachs of Columbia University's Earth Institute.[2]

Experts say ending hunger would be relatively inexpensive—basic health and nutrition for the world's poorest people could be met for an estimated $13 billion a year. Americans spend more than that annually on ice cream.

All around us there seems to be a metaphorical alignment of hopeful planets. Breakthroughs in communication, technology, agriculture and compassion are helping organizations and individuals address problems of poverty like never before. Incredible opportunities are emerging to do the work of Jesus—healing, feeding, clothing and caring, on a truly unprecedented scale.

This is the challenge of the 21st century.

And God is calling a 'Who me?' generation to rise to the occasion.

God is calling individuals as well as whole communities, faith communities, to gear up, recruit and re-tool—to grab hold of this emerging vision of God's Kingdom of healing and wholeness. It's breaking into our world like never before—maybe because our world is suffering like never before. The call of the Spirit may simply be the echoed cries of a wide world of millions of suffering people—let's take a few moments and look at the state of our world.

Poverty

"Without regard to race or religion, we will serve the needs of the poor and people on the verge of starvation" declared Episcopal Bishop Lloyd Allen of Honduras as he stood in front of a huge, nearly completed warehouse where he's overseeing a project that will funnel $35 million in goods and services each year to Honduras.[3]

> Help someone work their way out of poverty
>
> www.kiva.org

It's called 'Operation Sustaining Grace' and its headquarters are in a warehouse on a beautiful stretch of the sun-bathed Pacific Coast. It serves as a storage and distribution center for food, clothing, medicine, school supplies and other donated goods. Upwards of 150 communities throughout Honduras will benefit. Its food and milk programs already reach 200,000 children and seniors each year. Though one of the Episcopal Church's poorest, the Diocese of Honduras is also one of its fastest growing, opening, on average, more than two congregations a year for the last 30 years. "Actually," says Allen, "we have 28 communities on a waiting list, who have asked us to come out and minister to them. We will answer their call when we can provide trained clergy."

Unfortunately the depth of poverty and suffering that Bishop Allen is addressing is all too common—the need vastly outweighs the resources:

Nearly one half of the world, or three billion people, live on
> two dollars a day or less - one third of those, one billion people, live on a dollar a day or less.

40,000 children die every day of poverty.

Three-quarters of those, 30,000 children, die of utterly preventable
> diseases (such as mosquito bites and unclean drinking water).

One billion people can't write their own name.

This kind of poverty is not only mind-numbing but is simply unimaginable to most people in the western world. Due to the amazing prosperity we enjoy, the needs of the world's desperately poor are difficult for most of us to comprehend.

"By any objective criterion, the five percent of the world's people who live in the United States are an incredibly rich aristocracy... our standard of living... is at least as luxurious as was the lifestyle of the medieval aristocracy compared with their serfs."[4]

Indeed, more Americans die of obesity than starvation.

This is not to say that America doesn't have poverty issues of its own. Census numbers tell us that 37 million Americans are living in poverty and more than one-third of those are children.

> How rich are you compared to the rest of the world?
>
> Go to www.globalrichlist.com to find out

The highest percentages of our poor young people live in urban areas like Detroit where nearly one half of the children live in poverty. The U.S. Census defines the poverty threshold at $19,806 annual income or less for a family of four. This is problematic in itself because a family of four would have trouble making ends meet even if that number were doubled. This means, as the U.S. Conference of Mayors annually reports, that more and more Americans are asking for emergency food and shelter in our big cities each year. Low paying jobs and homelessness are the top causes.

Disease

Making matters worse is the brutal unfairness of disease.

The world's deadliest are AIDS, tuberculosis, and malaria.

These disproportionately afflict the poorest of the world's poor especially those in sub-Saharan Africa.

Take a grandmother named Marta who lives in a mud hut in the Northern Namibian bush. Marta, her daughter, and at least one of her grandchildren suffer from AIDS. Marta's body is also wracked with tuberculosis, which is an incurable affliction common to AIDS sufferers. Her treatment depends on a home-based care nurse from nearby St. Mary's Health Center. "HIV/AIDS is just everywhere," says Namibia's Bishop Suffragan Petrus Hilukilua. He finds that during Confirmation visits at local parishes, "You are often told that there are 'so many' candidates [but when you arrive you find] that one died or several died days ago so you have an unhappy service really."

The AIDS crisis is one of the most destructive epidemics in history.

AIDS has infected 40 million people worldwide,
    65% live in sub-Saharan Africa

. 5% are children.

Every day more than 1,400 newborns are infected
    with the HIV virus at birth.

This year about 5 million people will contract AIDS—
    the vast majority live in areas like Namibia
    and are least equipped to provide adequate treatment.

In the United States

40,000 people per year continue to be infected with HIV/AIDS.

73% of them are men,
    65% of them are African-American or Hispanic.

Thanks to medical advances a lot fewer Americans are dying of the disease. The mortality rate for people with AIDS declined 30% shortly after the turn of the millennium.

As in Marta's case a disease closely linked with AIDS is tuberculosis (TB). This is also most common in poor areas of Africa and Asia. TB kills about two million people per year though, unlike AIDS, it is curable. An unbelievable one third of the world's population carries the bacterium that causes TB. One in ten of these people will contract the disease sometime during their lives. Tuberculosis is growing. It's an airborne disease. It's very contagious. In fact, one active TB patient will infect 10-15 people every year.

Buy a Mosquito net,
save a life.
www.nothingbutnets.net

Malaria is the world's third deadliest disease. Mosquitoes carry it. It infects a total of 300 million people every year. One million people die from Malaria every year. 90% of its victims are in sub-Saharan Africa. It's estimated the disease costs the continent $12 billion in lost Gross National Product. The irony is that treatment and prevention, like inexpensive, insecticide-treated sleeping tents, would cost much less.

On a grand scale, poverty and disease are the most pressing problems of our age. Period. We can't give them too much attention.

History will praise or scorn our generation depending on our response to these challenges.

But depending on who you are and where you live, these problems may seem distant. Violence, racism, physical and sexual abuse, drugs and alcohol, gambling, pornography, urban decay, loneliness, depression, or a host of other difficulties could be playing much more important roles in your life.

Our litany of worries is as close as the daily newspaper, which, unfortunately, is never short of the stuff of which headlines are made.

The Frozen Chosen Thaw Out

Fortunately these problems aren't the only things making headlines.

Episcopal Relief and Development

ERD (www.er-d.org) is the main relief organization of the Episco-pal Church. In addition to providing ongoing support to worthy projects, it also provides emergency relief when disaster strikes.

While the average charitable organization spends twenty cents of each dollar on administration, ERD spends just seven cents of each dollar on administration.

We often read about the people and organizations working to solve them as well - like the Salvation Army, the Red Crescent Society, Doctors Without Borders, Mercy Corps, Episcopal Relief and Development and one of my favorites, the ONE Campaign. There are thousands of others - I thank God for everyone everywhere who is helping to bring healing and wholeness to our weary world. God uses religious people—God uses atheists—God uses everybody. And very frequently, the only thing they have in common is that at one point or another they asked the same question; 'Who me?'

This includes the Episcopal Church.

Like many established churches, we were once referred to as 'the frozen chosen' – a church many people characterized as being more concerned with its own preservation and somewhat removed from the needs of God's world. Many people wrote us off as a dwindling group of naval-gazing liberals, hopelessly asleep in the Light. But like many churches, we are re-awakening to the possibilities of a more challenging and authentic Christian life. Today, like never before, the Episcopal Church is on the move —and asking, 'Who me?'

We're asking this because through our prayers and worship, we hear the Lord inviting us to play our part in taking on the tremendous challenges before us. We also hear the Spirit's voice reawakening us to the tremendous gifts that God has given us. Episcopalians are realizing anew that God sees tremendous potential in us:

God sees us passionately devoted to the Gospel of Jesus Christ.

God sees us willing to fight poverty, disease and injustice.

God sees us as thinkers.

God sees us as accepting and open-minded.

God sees us as reconcilers and forgivers.

God sees us forming faithful and inclusive communities.

God sees us as upholders of valuable traditions.

God sees us devoted to the Eucharist.

God sees us offering helpful missionary opportunities.

God sees that we have good news to share.

We all know that you don't have to be an Episcopalian to help solve the world's problems—religious people have never had a corner on morality. But God is using the Episcopal Church to accomplish work that desperately needs to be done—to feed, to heal and to reconcile a hurting world that is just waiting for us to do our part.

Yes, the Lord is up to some earth-shaking changes.

And we want to be part of it.

No, we're not all of it.
And we're certainly not in charge of it.
But we're strapping ourselves in, packing a big lunch, and pinching ourselves, joining every saint and prophet who's preceded us, as we continually ask: 'Who me?'

2. TRANSITION

"It's not having what you want—It's wanting what you've got."
Sheryl Crow

Sifting

Every Sunday evening my friend Jack leads a group of a half dozen or so Christians in an intensive graduate-level course—it's called EFM—it stands for 'Education for Ministry' (more on page 83)—but since they begin their meetings with a huge potluck, Jack tells me it really stands for 'Eating for Ministry.'

Once the dishes are done and the meeting gets going somebody stands up and gives something called a 'theological reflection.' This is an elaborate way of doing one of the most important things anybody can do: looking at your life.

Theological reflections answer basic questions like: what is the Holy Spirit up to in my world? How has the Spirit taken root in the souls and actions of those around me? Where has the Spirit taken me? Where is the Lord leading me now? Theological reflections use the Bible and the gathered community to help people sort out and make sense of their complicated lives.

Theological reflection is a Christian way of sifting.

What I mean by sifting is the conscious act of making important distinctions regarding the influencers in our lives. It's a mental exercise we all participate in everyday.

Sifting is naming those things that are essential and naming those things that aren't. It comes to play when we decide what to read, what to buy, what to listen to—essentially everything that we have a choice about letting into our heads.

If we don't sift, we drift.

Most of us know the remarkable opportunities we have to change the world. We know they're right in front of us. We know they're doable.

So why don't we... just do it?

It's because we live in a time that makes this kind of work really, really hard. There are huge forces at work that keep us sidetracked and sedated, daydreaming and distracted—while the Spirit pulls us one way, a billion different things pull us another.

So before we get too far into the nuts and bolts of the Episcopal Church, let's look at the state of the Church in North America to help us see why my tradition can be a particularly helpful one.

As we will see, North American Christianity is in a rather well entrenched period of transition.

And it requires us to do some serious sifting.

Fiddling

I remember reading somewhere that the Roman emperor Nero played his violin while Rome burned about two thousand years ago.

That's because he was insane.

Well, today we could argue that you and I, and much of the Western world are doing the same thing—we preoccupy ourselves with entertainments and diversions while much of the world fights to stay alive.

And like Nero, we also have an excuse. We lead complex and stressful lives, full of scary uncertainties—lives we might even call, 'insane.'
We don't often consider the big picture because we don't have time to.

We're in a hurry.
We're impatient.
We just can't seem to do one thing at a time.

TVs offer us 'Picture in a Picture.'
Work-out machines have magazine racks.
New cars offer built-in cell phones.
Studies say people may pack the equivalent of 31 hours of activities into a 24-hour day by multi-tasking.

We work on average one month more each year than we did 35 years ago. We sleep 20% less than we did one hundred years ago. In fact, sleep clinics in America tripled in the last decade of the 20th century.

The last one hundred years has given us more technological advancements than the previous millennium. And the last decade has given us more of these breakthroughs than the previous century.

Today, the pace of Western advancement has reached such a clip that technologists say one year is equivalent to a decade. Many American businesses no longer waste time on ten-year plans, even five-year plans are considered speculative.

Yet despite our progress we're still struggling.

A generation or so ago an average American breadwinner could pay for housing, transportation, taxes and health insurance on 54% of his income. Today, to cover all of those expenses, plus the cost of childcare (because two people now work), it takes 74% of our income. America's median hourly wage is barely higher than it was 35 years ago, adjusted for inflation. The income of a man in his 30s is now 12 percent below that of a man his age three decades ago.[1] We're working much harder and, in real dollars, we're making much less.

Modern life, with all its advancements, has put too many of us on endless treadmills that totally drain us—its demands are keeping us up too late and waking us up too early.

Who's got the time and energy to sift through all this stuff?

We don't.

We barely have time to think.
So many of us don't.

Here's where we are:

52% of Americans believe in astrology.

42% believe in communication with the dead.

53% believe God created humans in their present form exactly
as described in the Bible

When visitors take a helicopter tour of the Grand Canyon their guides
routinely describe, without judgment either way, two accounts of
the canyon's origins—one is based on geology; the other describes
the possibility that the whole thing came about after 40 days
and 40 nights of rain.

Anthropologist Thomas de Zengotita dares us to take a poll of any graduate school humanities class, asking how many people believe in paranormal phenomena or alien abduction.[2] If they're honest their responses won't differ much from an average Oprah audience. "They won't, for the most part, affirm a definite belief, but they won't want to issue any blanket denials either. Maybe, they'll say, who knows? Who really knows anything?"

Religion professor Stephen Prothero says 'ditto.' His specialty is religious literacy in America, which, he has found, is nothing short of abysmal. Prothero says only 10% of our teenagers can name all five of the world's major religions. 15% can't name any of them. Nearly two-thirds of us believe the Bible holds the answers to all or most of life's basic questions yet only half of us can name even one of the four gospels. Prothero says most Americans can't name the first book in the Bible and 10% of us believe Joan of Arc was Noah's wife.[3]

We're a nation of very religious people who don't know very much about religion. We could chalk it up to what social scientists call 'the dumbing down of America.' And there's plenty of blame to go around:

an assaultive media,

an increase in the number of broken homes,

decreased parental contact, supervision, authority and control,

a lack of significant 'free time',

increased workplace demands and uncertainties.

All of these contribute to our waning abilities to talk, think, work, write and pay attention.

Sociologist Jane Healy sees it in the classroom. She says teachers have been forced to make class work and exams easier because parents and administrators are demanding better and better grades. She points to this study comparing reading tests given in 1964 and 1988: The 1964 exam went to average students and proved significantly more difficult than the 1988 exam, which was called an 'advanced' test.

And here's the kicker: the 1964 exam was for fourth graders.
The 1988 exam was for ninth graders.[4]

If you're like me you'd think our churches would see the problem. You'd think we'd be rolling up our sleeves and helping people sift through it all.

But we're not.

In fact, you might say we're making it worse.

The Largest 15
Christian Denominations
in the United States

Denomination name	Members (thousands)
Roman Catholic	67,821
Southern Baptist	16,267
United Methodist	8,186
Church of Latter Day Saints (Mormons)	5,999
Church of God in Christ	5,450
National Baptist Convention, USA	5,000
Evangelical Lutheran Church in America	4,930
National Baptist Convention of America	3,500
Presbyterian Church (USA)	3,189
Assemblies of God	2,779
African Methodist Episcopal Church	2,500
National Missionary Baptist Convention	2,500
Progressive National Baptist Convention	2,500
Lutheran Church—Missouri Synod	2,464
Episcopal Church	2,284

Source:
2006 Yearbook of American and Canadian Churches, National Council of Churches.

Today some 85% of Americans identify themselves as Christians—there are now more Christians in the U.S. than there have been in any other country in the history of the world.[5] Yet we all know our most conspicuous representation of our faith, the institutional Church, is largely viewed as irrelevant and out of step with reality.

The Church's opinions are rarely taken seriously.

We're more reactive than proactive.

Our most visible spokespersons are more often reduced to the barbs of late night comedy than they are asked to weigh in on important world issues.

Christianity in North America has a very serious image problem particularly among the young, according to pollster David Kinnaman.[6] His research shows an overwhelming percentage of those outside the Church, aged sixteen to twenty-nine years old, view Christians with hostility, resentment and disdain.

Here's how they describe us:

Anti-homosexual 91%

Judgmental 87%

Hypocritical 85%

Old-Fashioned 78%

Too Political 75%

Out of touch with reality 72%

Insensitive to others 70%

Boring 68%

Kinnaman says it would be hard to overestimate, "how firmly people reject—and feel rejected by—Christians." Or think about it another way, when you're introduced to a friend, neighbor or business associate who's not a Christian you may as well have it tattooed on your forehead: "Anti-gay, Hypocritical, Judger." We may not think of ourselves like this, but other people do.

Maybe it's because many Christians are out of touch with Jesus' central message and have grown out of touch with core Christian virtues like humility, kindness and forgiveness. Not knowing the Bible very well, perhaps we've lost touch with the main thrust of the Gospel message and tried to accommodate and compromise a message that really doesn't work very well when watered down.

Many of our churches have become more willing to buy into the American civil religion of manifest destiny, patriotism, and 'family values' than to take seriously the hard Gospel words of 'taking up the cross' and 'laying down your life.'

Take a look at any big city skyline.

The icons of commerce reign.
From the corporate headquarters to the shopping malls, they shamelessly proclaim America's real priorities.

What does it say about our 'Christian' society that there's rarely a church, social service agency, or other symbol of our faith of similar size and prestige?

What does it say that most of us have probably never heard this startling statistic: if every Christian in America gave just 10% of their income to feed the hungry, world poverty would be history?

Instead, religion critics say most Christians have embraced America's secular free-market passion without asking important questions.

We see this in church services that offer a me-centered Gospel, where feeling good and 'getting my needs met' are top priorities. Pop psychology has elbowed biblical exegesis out of the pulpit. No big surprise as self-help books now outsell theological books in most Christian book-stores.[7] One sociologist calls it the triumph of the therapeutic.

Today's Gospel is often reduced to a message focused on individual salvation—the fundamental question is the self-centered: 'Am I saved?' In too many churches the process of making disciples has turned into spiritual and religious exercises that deal with personal salvation— we've separated the gift of God in Christ from the reason it was given to us: to empower us in word and deed to be Christ's disciples to the world.

When the stereotypical country preacher shouted, 'We're saved to serve!' I'm pretty sure he meant Christians were supposed to serve people other than themselves.

Creating communities that form conspicuous lives of self-sacrifice, reconcili-ation and service seem harder and harder to find.

And to be fair, the job of simply being the Church is enormous.
The impact our society has on our congregations can't be overstated.
We face incredible even irresistible temptations to buy into our culture.
Our world defines us by our economic worth and by our accumulation of experiences and things.

Advertising seemingly envelops us at every corner. Its job isn't to inform us, it's to create a desire within us to consume. Astoundingly, it convinces an already affluent society that we simply don't have enough to survive in modest comfort. Luxuries are constantly being re-classified as necessities. We now spend more money each year on advertising than we do on all our public institutions of higher education. Few can argue with one expert's assessment: our "increasing affluent standard of living is the god of the twenty first century North America, and the adman is its prophet."[8]

We minister in a society where our primary public policy is to increase personal and national wealth—not to help us love God and love our neighbors. One commentator says, "When a church's theology holds up a vision for swimming upstream—and most of that church's members are floating downstream on yachts—something's got to give. [Usually] it's the theology that gets sold away, not the yachts."[9]

It's become very difficult to live up to the Bible's description of Christianity.

Activist Jim Wallis likes to tell the story about his first year in seminary when he and some other students decided to go through the Bible verse by verse and cut out every reference that talked about the poor, wealth, poverty, injustice and oppression, and God's response to these.

Wallis says they found thousands of verses.

In fact, this was the second most prominent theme in the Old Testament (the first was idolatry, and the two are often related).

In the New Testament, one in every 16 verses deals with these subjects.
In the first three Gospels it's one in ten verses.
In the book of Luke it's one in seven.

Wallis' story begs the question: What kind of sifting are we doing? How come we're letting all the important stuff fall through the cracks? What's keeping us from keeping the main thing, the main thing?

Transition

The short answer is that Christianity in North America is confused and in the throes of a major transition. It's not what it once was nor does it seem to know what it wants to be. We're kind of like kids on a merry-go-round that's going too fast.

And we can't get off.

So most of our energy is focused on simply holding on.

Systemic membership declines, which have hit long-established churches first (like the Episcopal Church), continue to spread. America's largest protestant denomination, the Southern Baptist convention, publicly worries about its future. Even with the wave of Latino immigration, the Roman Catholic Church is closing parishes. Our best and brightest aren't going to seminary any more—many are heading for Hollywood, Madison Avenue and Wall Street instead.

Most Americans fear neither social ostracism nor eternal damnation when they skip Sunday mornings at church. Are we surprised that the focus of most of our churches isn't on Gospel issues of poverty, injustice and making the world a better place—but on survival?

Theologian Alex Roxburgh likes to use the picture below.

It shows us three eras, Pre-Constantinian (0-315 CE), Christendom (Middle Ages), Post-Christendom (Today).

In the first few hundred years of Christianity the Church stood outside the dominant seat of culture. The arrows show how this small group exerted influence. Then, as Christianity grew and spread and was adopted by the dominant world powers, its influence spread from inside out. Today, the Church is no longer a political powerhouse and, in too many places, no longer has a significant impact on the dominant power structures. "Confused and uncertain," writes Roxburgh, "the church today is more likely to be concerned about its own future than its influence; security and survival have priority over missional engagement with our postmodern culture."[10]

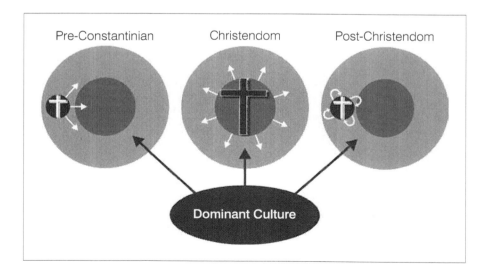

All we need to do is look at all the scandals and arguments that are rocking our churches—from human sexuality to church government and everything in between. We've let our fights take center stage.

Of course doctrine and discipline need to be dealt with. But this constant preoccupation has effectively given us laryngitis.

We've lost our voice. We've drifted into irrelevance.

One critic says, "You've got self-righteous people on all sides arguing with other self-righteous people. God is saying 'No' to … these little trivial debates we're having in the church while hundreds of thousands of people are starving to death."[11]

Don't we know that few people outside our congregations care?

Well, we're finding out.

A lot of us go to church because we want to develop spiritually in the context of the Gospel and a Christian community.

We don't come to fight about who's right and who's wrong. We come to hear about the message of Jesus. We're hungry to find an honest environment where we can grow in spiritual knowledge and learn how Jesus helps us help ourselves and others.

And God is hearing our prayers.

Renewal

My church, like everyone else's, is making a difficult transition into the 21st century. A lot of sifting is being done.

As I mentioned previously, like almost every mainline Protestant church we're recovering from a lapse in Christian vitality. For a wide variety of reasons, in the latter years of the 20th century, we've turned inward and had trouble keeping focus on our Christian mission. One expert says we became complacent and we got off track:

"Many mainstream congregations became a kind of Christian version of the Rotary Club, understanding the church as a religious place for social acceptability and business connections. In a very real way, mainline Protestants retained the ideal of comprehensiveness while jettisoning the idea that people are spiritually sick and need healing. Everyone was welcome—with no spiritual demands other than to conform to some sort of generalized Protestant morality. As a result, many mainline congregations forgot the practices that originally formed their traditions, making participation in their churches optional at best and irrelevant at worst... [By the time the 1970s rolled in] the church was an extension of post-war, middle-class aspirations, run by bureaucracies in the faith business."[12]

The major problem here is that Jesus didn't come to earth to start a faith business. Jesus didn't come to support the Establishment.

Jesus had no intention of setting up bureaucracies.

Jesus came to shatter the power structure and change the way we think.

Jesus came to start a revolution.

What Jesus said was so powerful that people literally dropped what they were doing and followed him.

Jesus' message was so attractive that people sold everything they had to practice what he taught—and minister to the poor, suffering and afflicted.

Historians tell us that Jesus has affected our planet more than anyone in the history of the world.

Jesus started a counterinsurgency based on love, mercy, inclusion and forgiveness, and was executed for it.

And Jesus asked his followers to take the same actions—to reach beyond themselves.

It is amazing that anyone would follow.

But over two millennia, billions have. At least we've tried.

History books record the stories of our successes and failures.

God's Church goes up and down in its faithfulness.

When some parts struggle, other parts take off.

We evolve in fits and starts.

And now God seems fit to give us a new start.

Tool Box

The Episcopal Church's renewal can only be based on the Gospel of Jesus Christ and our devotion to following His words and example no matter what the cost. Historically, no other foundation has helped Christians serve the world more effectively.

The Episcopal Church

- 6,900 parishes
- Average Sunday attendance at an average parish—129 people
- 1.6 million members
- 52% of churches built before 1950
- One of the 44 national and regional churches that make up the Anglican Communion (80 million members)
- Clergy are called Deacons, Priests and Bishops
- Clergy are male and female
- Male priests are called 'Father' or The Rev.
- Female priests are called 'Mother' or The Rev.
- The word 'Episcopal' is an adjective as in The Episcopal Church. The word 'Episcopalian' is a noun. A person is an Episcopalian, but does not attend an Episcopalian Church.

Episcopalians go about building this foundation with a very distinctive, old toolbox. It's been handed down to us by generations and generations of people who have honed, polished and perfected the valuable tools it contains. They are tools like reason, reconciliation, moderation, openness, acceptance, inclusion, and tradition.

Of course we Episcopalians are not the only ones with these tools, but we are unique in the way we use them.

We want to use them to join the Lord's Ongoing Worldwide Terrestrial Rehab Project.

We want to put our gifts to work to help correct injustices in our communities and in the world beyond. We want to do our part to help build a kingdom of healing, mercy, justice and peace that is possible when we choose the path of God. And we want to share them with anyone and everyone who would like them.

In the chapters ahead we will take a closer look at these tools and the distinctive ways that Episcopalians use them.

We know that the Lord is doing some serious Kingdom-building.

That's why we're bringing our toolbox.

3. THINK

"Anglicanism stands not for tolerance
for the sake of compromise
but for comprehension for the sake of truth."

Former Archbishop of York, Dr. Cyril F. Garbett

Think

Years ago when I lived in California I used to hang out with a small group of Christians from my parish. We met twice a month for coffee, bagels, and more than a little time studying the Bible.

One morning we were sitting around my living room talking about how we'd stumbled into the Episcopal Church (70% of Episcopalians are converts). Roberta was there—she's a journalist—a street reporter—and no pushover. I'll never forget how she explained it.

Roberta said the reason she joined the Episcopal Church was because of all the Christians she knew Episcopalians were the least annoying.

We all snickered
—mainly because we all knew plenty of annoying Episcopalians.

But at the heart of her comment I think she was trying to say she had found a place where she could be herself. She'd found a place where she didn't feel judged. She'd found a place that was open and accepting to her as she struggled to make sense of what God was up to in her life.

But most of all I think Roberta, the interrogator, had found a place where she could to do one of the really important things God had created her to do: ask questions.

Few people can argue that one of God's greatest gifts is curiosity.
We can ask questions.
We can debate the answers.
We can reason.

As we've marched through time our thirst for knowledge has turned into a mind-blowing array of discoveries. Just look at the things we've dreamed up—the printing press, Silly String, the internal combustion engine, Jiffy Pop, tummy tucks, even disco.

Yet for some reason Christianity is much better known for its suspicion rather than its celebration of reason. Many Christians who are rightfully concerned with the inimical effects of a fallen world have tended to look at the wider culture with more skepticism than appreciation. For two millennia Christians have dwelled rather uncomfortably in a place of genuine tension between a love for a world God created and called "good," and a world where sin and death have free reign.

In a culture that's growing increasingly complex and complicated, burying our heads in religious sand piles is not good for us, or for the world. Sandy ears make it hard to think (plus, they itch).

And the Lord wants us to think.

This is something my church has helped me do. The Episcopal Church has helped me answer questions by letting me ask them.

My church has long been known for its studied belief that all of Creation is God's Creation—and it's good, very good.

The gifts of reason and intellect were created by God and for God's glory.

Of course, Episcopalians aren't the only ones who believe this.
But we wish more people did.

Mainly because there are a lot of thinking people around like Roberta, who are looking for safe places to ask their questions, figure out their answers, and know that God is smack dab in the middle of it all.

> Faith and inquiry
> are welcome at:
> www.explorefaith.org
> or
> www.beliefnet.org

A Reason to Adore

Not long ago I went to Utah with a dozen rowdy teenagers from my church.

No, I didn't lose a bet—we were on a pilgrimage.

We went deep into the desert to search for a God we all knew was already with us. As we trekked through the empty desert, hiking trails and climbing mountains, we knew we weren't the first European-Americans there. The Mormons had been there before us in 1847. And soon after that, a bishop from the Episcopal Church joined them.

Unlike the other non-Mormon ministers who preceded him, he was welcomed, and he stayed. It's a good thing because Bishop Daniel Tuttle would do some important work and say some important things about faith and reason.

Tuttle was sent out as a missionary bishop to Montana, Idaho and Utah in 1867. He'd been contacted by a handful of non-Mormons who wanted him to set up a church in Salt Lake City. They wanted somebody who wouldn't pick fights with the Mormons, but at the same time would also stand up for their convictions.

They wanted somebody who could help them articulate what it is they believed in a respectful and rational way.

So Bishop Tuttle signed up. He was well-educated and well-spoken. He understood the qualities of reason, logic and human ingenuity. He saw these as expressions of God's handiwork, meant for the greater good of the world.

During his many meetings with Mormon friends and neighbors he frequently appealed to reason as an integral part of his faith. He understood the thorough examination of what it is we believe as a central part of who it is we want to be—people who live authentic lives.

He said this:

"We have a faith not afraid to reason and a reason not ashamed to adore."

Bishop Tuttle believed that as bodies are meant to be exercised, minds are meant to be used, stretched, challenged, and to become all that they can be. While Tuttle did not agree with the Mormon religion, he was wise enough to treat his neighbors with kindness and respect and to maintain courteous relations. He preached and lived the Golden Rule to 'do unto others as you would have them do unto you.'

Bishop Tuttle became the first and most highly regarded non-Mormon to establish a religious institution in Utah. Decades after he died, the president of the Mormon Church thanked him, "He went east and told the truth about us, that we were 'a God-fearing, upright, conscientious people, serving God.' While he did not agree with us he admired our integrity."

Tripod

If Bishop Tuttle were around today he'd remind us that Episcopalians balance their beliefs on something like a camera tri-pod. The three legs are the Bible, tradition and common sense (often referred to as "reason").

In general, the first leg is centered on what the New Testament says, the second is what the Christian consensus has always tended to be, and the third is what works and rings true to our own day-by-day experience of God's activity in Creation.[1]

Like a tri-pod, all three are needed to achieve balance —if one leg keels over, the camera goes down and you are out of business.

As a way to arrive at truth, Episcopalians believe common sense is simply irreplaceable (we'll talk about the Bible and tradition later on). It helps us interpret Scripture and tradition. It allows itself to be corrected and enlightened by them.

Common sense is more than just raw calculation, cold logic or the distillation of subjective life experience.

Tripod Forms Traditions

Visit different Episcopal churches and you may notice subtle distinctions in ritual, architecture, and liturgy. These preferences in churchmanship are commonly termed **high, low** or **broad**. In general, these refer to which leg of the tripod a parish leans toward.

Anglo-Catholic, or high churches emphasize tradition, hence our catholic heritage, seen in the prominence of formal liturgy (smells & bells), crucifixes and the sacraments.

Evangelical, or low churches emphasize Scripture and our protestant heritage. Worship is characterized by subjective piety, personal conversion and un-elaborate church decor.

Liberal, or broad churches, stress reason. Traditionally indifferent to doctrine and liturgy, these churches may or may not use traditional forms of ritual or decor.

Most parishes fall somewhere in-between one, two or all three of these.[3]

Rather, it draws upon the entirety of human understanding and experience and helps us figure out what we should do in any given situation.[2]

Of course this doesn't mean common sense is infallible. We know it is. But while human reasoning can corrupt and distort, Episcopalians are quick to point out that our intelligence can also lead us into deeper truth and understanding of God and God's mysterious ways.

Episcopalians believe that while rationalism—the sole dependence on our intellectual faculties—is a sin, so too is anti-intellectualism which discounts the mind's capabilities and leaves life's most important decisions up to superstition and blind faith.

This is why Episcopalians are often big supporters of education.
In fact, a lot of us are teachers.

The founding of some of the most prestigious universities and colleges in England and the United States can be linked to a Christian conviction that God comes to us not simply through the Bible and tradition, but through the application of our intellects. We share in the heritage of many of our country's most distinguished learning institutions. They came into being because of this high regard for not only the gift of intelligence, but also the responsibility God gives to us to develop our gifts and use them for the greater good of the world.

Blinded Me With Science

One way Episcopalians live out these convictions is by having open and substantive conversations with science. Most Episcopalians would agree that science and religion are not opposed to each other, but are actually intellectual, "cousins under the skin."

One of my seminary professors liked to say it this way:

Suppose you walk into a kitchen and see two people watching a steaming teakettle on a stove.

"What's going on?" you ask.

The first person, a scientist, says, "That's easy. The ignited natural gas is in contact with the metal teapot, which in turn is forcing the water molecules to go through a dramatic change which will soon drive steam through the spout and create a rather loud whistling sound."

While this is certainly true, her answer is much different than the second persons'. She's a priest.

She answers the question, 'What's going on?' with the simple response, "I want a cup of tea."

In other words, science and religion are fundamentally engaged, in different ways, in a search for truth, "Both are searching for motivated belief.

Neither can claim absolute certain knowledge, for each must base its conclusions on an interplay between interpretation and experience. In consequence, both must be open to the possibility of correction. Neither deals simply with mere fact or mere opinion. They are both part of the great human endeavor to understand."[4]

Our beliefs about reason ask us to take seriously our search for knowledge and truth in the face of what I described in the last chapter as our utterly schizophrenic culture—one that wants to possess the latest technical discoveries while holding onto a grade school level faith.

It's absolutely necessary that the Church re-claim the rightful place of reason and intellectual pursuit in its faith communities. We need a way of being Christian that's open to the increasingly complex ways in which we arrive at truth.

We need a framework that allows us freedom to live authentically with life's ambiguities realizing that honest inquiry is a way of faithful living.

We need to realize that the maturation of our minds is inextricably linked to the salvation of our souls.

The Faith of Charles Darwin

Charles Darwin was baptized an Anglican. He attended a Church of England school and studied theology with the in-tention of becoming a priest. In latter years his faith became more nominal. But his devotion to inquiry and the search for truth provide a lasting legacy to the importance of critical examination and experimentation as a Christian discipline.

These convictions have led many Episcopalians to get involved in substantive and ongoing conversations with scientists and theologians in a variety of areas. It has also helped us make more informed decisions on policy stances the Church has taken (more on page 138). Our interest in science has led us to write books, articles and even science curriculums. Here's a portion of one of those curriculums that gives us an idea of what some Episcopalians are saying about science[5]:

Does the Bible teach science?
Do we find scientific knowledge in the Bible?
Episcopalians believe that the Bible "contains all things necessary to salvation" (Book of Common Prayer, p. 868): it is the inspired and authoritative source of truth about God, Christ, and the Christian life. John Polkinghorne, following sixteenth-century Anglican theologian Richard Hooker, reminds us Anglicans and Episcopalians that the Bible does not contain all necessary truths about everything else. The Bible, including Genesis, is not a divinely dictated scientific textbook. We discover scientific knowledge about God's universe in nature not Scripture.

Does Big Bang cosmology prove the doctrine of creation out of nothing?
No. Big Bang cosmology seems to be in tune with both the concepts of creation out of nothing and continuous creation. However, theology does not depend upon science to verify its doctrines, just as science does not depend upon theology to verify its theories. However, science can inspire theology to think new thoughts about the relationship between God and the creation, as Big Bang cosmology and evolution have done.

Is it proper to speak of an evolving creation?
Yes. When astronomers look out into space they look back in time. Thus, they are able to see our universe at many stages of cosmic evolution

Prayer from the Society
of Ordained Scientists

Almighty God,
Creator and Redeemer of all that is,
source and foundation
of time and space, matter and energy,
life and consciousness;
grant to all who study
the mysteries of your creation,
grace to be true witnesses
to your glory
and faithful stewards of your gifts;
through Jesus Christ our Lord.

Amen

since its beginning in the Big Bang. Here on earth biologists, geneticists, paleontologists, and other scientists are showing that life has evolved over four billion years, and are reconstructing evolution's history. None of these scientific discoveries and the theories that explain them stands in conflict with what the Bible reveals about God's relationship to the creation.

What are theologians saying about God's creating activities in light of modern scientific discoveries and theories?

While theologians have proposed different models of how God acts in an evolving world, they agree that God is best understood as interacting with the world rather than intervening in it—a God intimately present in the world (as Scripture also reveals) rather than a God "out there." According to the late Anglican priest and biologist Arthur Peacocke, God acts as Creator "in, with and under" the natural processes of chance and natural selection. Theologian Elizabeth Johnson writes that God uses random genetic mutations to ensure variety, resilience, novelty and freedom in the world. At the same time, the universe operates by certain natural laws or "secondary causes" by which God, the Primary Cause, ensures regularity and reliability in nature. Physicist and theologian Howard Van Till writes that God has creatively and generously given the creation all of the powers and capacities "in the beginning" that enable it to organize and transform itself into the variety of atoms, molecules, chemical elements, galaxies, stars, and planets in the universe, and species of living things on this earth. In this evolving universe, God does not dictate the outcome of nature's activities, but allows the world to become what it is able to become in all of its diversity: one could say that God has a purpose rather than a fixed plan, a goal rather than a blueprint. As the nineteenth-century Anglican minister Charles Kingsley put it, God has made a world that is able to make itself. Polkinghorne states that God has given the world a free process, just as God has given human beings free choice. Divine Love (1 John 4:8) frees the universe and life to develop as they are able to by using all of their divinely given powers and capacities. The universe, as Augustine of Hippo said in the fourth century, is "God's love song." Because God's Love is poured out within the creation, theologian Denis Edwards asserts that "the Trinitarian God is present to every creature in its being and becoming." These are but some of the concepts that contemporary theologians are offering to account for God's relationship to an evolving creation.

While the Episcopal Church has never officially spoken on evolution or intelligent design we have broadly accepted evolution from Darwin's time to now. Our General Convention has passed a resolution affirming the ability of God to create in any form and fashion, which would include evolution.

Anglicans and Episcopalians, some of whom are both theologians and scientists, continue to contribute to the development of new theories and theologies of an evolving creation.

This is something we seem to learn more and more about each day.

Heavenly Host

One of my earliest childhood memories is sitting in front of the black and white TV in my parent's bedroom and watching the Apollo 11 space mission. While my brothers and I sat bug-eyed looking at Neil Armstrong and Buzz Aldrin bounce around on the moon and collect space rocks, little did we know that something even more amazing was happening.

On Sunday, July 20, 1969 Buzz Aldrin, a devout Christian, celebrated the Holy Eucharist on the moon.

That's right—he had communion—inside that tiny space capsule.

And he didn't use Space Food Sticks and Tang.
Aldrin packed a stash of bread and wine.

The word 'Eucharist' is Greek and it means thanksgiving.
For most Christians, the Eucharist is the supreme way we give thanks.

Buzz Aldrin was a top-notch scientist and astronaut.

Like many of his contemporaries, including Episcopalians Frank Borman, Jim Lovell and Al Worden, I'm sure he wrestled with questions about science and religion just like you and I do.

But what his 'cosmic communion' tells me is that he found a way to see his gifts of intellectual curiosity and scientific inquiry flourish while still embracing that mysterious part of him that yearned for spiritual fulfillment.

Buzz Aldrin's outer-space sacrament gives me hope. It tells me that there are faith communities out there where it's OK for me to ask real questions about the real world around me. And if I don't get all the answers, it's OK.

God is there.

God's people are there.

I don't struggle alone.

Of course the Episcopal Church isn't the only place where questions are welcome.

We're one of many places that strive to be in conversation with our amazing, beautiful, scary, complicated, magical, inviting, mysterious and dangerous world.

We see inquiry as a God-given characteristic of who we're meant to be.

We are hard-wired to ask questions and when we do, we become more like we were meant to be.

Christians need the scientist and minister.

We need the microscope and the Manuscript. These

Cosmic Communion

Lunar Module pilot Edwin "Buzz" Aldrin packed something special in his lunch box… bread and wine to celebrate Communion on the moon. Due to political concerns, NASA kept this a secret for two decades until it came out in Aldrin's memoirs. With an earned doctorate from MIT, Col. Aldrin was acknowledged as the most highly educated of the first astronauts; a "true scientist," yet respected by peers as a devout Christian.

The first Holy Communion celebrated on the moon is significant in other ways:

- The first liquid poured in the Moon's 1/6th gravity was the Blood of Christ.

- The first food and drink consumed by humans on another celestial body was the Blessed Sacrament.

- The most remote act of worship (235,000 miles from Earth) ever undertaken was a celebration of Jesus Christ's death and resurrection.[6]

are things that make us think.

And that's not just a good thing, it's a God thing.

4. WELCOME

"[The Episcopal Church] is the roomiest Church in Christendom…
it accepts the basic facts of Christian faith
as symbols of transparent truths, which each may interpret
as his or her insight explores their depth and wonder.

If its spirit and attitude were better understood,
it would be once the haven and the home of many vexed minds
torn between loyalty to the old faith and the new truth."

A convert to the Episcopal Church

Welcome

One of my good friends says this is her favorite joke—a Baptist minister, a Catholic priest and an Episcopal priest arrived in heaven and stood in front of St. Peter at the Pearly Gates.

"I'll let you in," said Peter, "only if you can give me the correct answer to this question: Who do you say Jesus Christ of Nazareth is?"

The three ministers scratched their heads. First, the Baptist spoke up. "Well," he said, "the Bible says…" St. Peter immediately interrupted. "I'm sorry, but perhaps you didn't understand the question, I asked who do YOU say that Jesus is? You can't come into heaven."

The Catholic priest then spoke up. "Well," he said, "the Pope says…" Again, St. Peter interrupted, "I'm sorry, but I asked you who do YOU say that Jesus is? You can't come into heaven either."

It was now up to the Episcopalian, who immediately chimed in and said, "Jesus of Nazareth is the only Son of God, the Holy One who came to redeem the world from sin and He is my Lord and Savior."

A smile drew across St. Peter's face.
Then just as he began to usher the priest into heaven she turned around and added, "But on the other hand…"

Maybe you've noticed, but Episcopalians have a reputation for looking at both sides of the coin. Many of us are curious and like to explore our options. Some people admire our fearlessness. They compliment us for our patience and evenhandedness. Others say we're unwilling to take a stand—a textbook case of the bland leading the bland.

A critical newspaper columnist once called us overeager to embrace, "whatever the liberal elements of secular society deem permissible or politically correct." But we think our hesitancy to make sweeping moral judgments and write out long lists of hard and fast rules is deeply rooted in a thoroughly biblical and historic faith.

We're actually in the dead center of a long line of Christian thought that believes one of the main thrusts of Jesus' message is acceptance, openness and inclusion. We see God's overriding attribute—love—made flesh and blood in Jesus Christ.

And Jesus is the host of the party whose first word is always, 'welcome.'

Rudder

Not long ago a news story described a State Supreme Court justice who really loved the Ten Commandments. One of the first things he did after taking office was literally to set his beliefs in stone for all to see.

Just as he had previously displayed the Ten Commandments in his courtroom, he put up a two and a half ton granite monument of the Commandments in the state judicial building's rotunda. He kicked off a legal battle over religion's place in the public arena. The media descended in droves. "God has chosen this time and this place so we can save our country and save our courts for our children" the judge told CNN.[1]

After he was dismissed from the bench for not taking down the monument, he began criss-crossing the country with his 'rock.'

The judge and the rock appeared at rallies, churches and shopping malls. Passing drivers would pull alongside the semi hauling the rock, honk and give a thumbs-up.

A religious chord was struck. 77% of Americans had not been in favor of removing the monument from public property. They apparently had no problem with this kind of moralism.

This judge, like many of us, was disheartened over the loss of religion's prominence in today's culture. And he tried to turn the situation around.

Many of us hearken back to the days when school prayer was acceptable, divorce rates were lower and the economic climate allowed one spouse to stay at home and raise the kids without risking financial hardship. (Of course those 'good old days' were anything but good for blacks who used separate restrooms, and to whom non-menial jobs were closed; gays and lesbians who were socially ostracized; and the majority of women whose opportunities outside the home were limited at best.)

The removal of that monument is a social indicator of the winding down of a religious era in North America.

It's a transition that's been going on for years and just when it'll end is anybody's guess.

What's more important is how we deal with it.

In times like these we all yearn for stability. But do we find it by pounding ever deeper into the sea floor the moorings of our own particular religious convictions? Or are we willing to take a chance and untie our ships from our well-anchored preconceptions and use our faith to steer?

How do we see our faith?

Anchor or rudder?

Most Episcopalians believe the 'Good News' of the Gospel is about something much deeper than the moralism behind public lobbying for issues like the Ten Commandments.

It's about something more fluid that takes us to the core of liberty, freedom, forgiveness, and salvation. Most Episcopalians respect people's rights to say and do what they want,but we tend to avoid making these kinds of sweeping, public moral pronouncements.

It's not because we don't believe the Commandments. It's because we Episcopalians, like many Christians, believe the primary message of the Gospel is the forgiveness of sins and reconciliation of the penitent.

We believe this is at the heart of what Jesus taught and lived.

Forgiveness

After Jesus rose from the dead, the book of Luke tells us that Christ appeared to the disciples.

He said, "Thus it is written, that the Messiah is to suffer and to rise from the dead on the third day, and that repentance and forgiveness of sins is to be proclaimed in his name to all nations." (Luke 24:46-47) Elsewhere in Luke, Jesus tells his followers, "Unless you repent you will all perish." (Luke 13:3) Further on, St. Peter says, "Repent, therefore and turn to God so that your sins may be wiped out." (Acts 3:19) In the stories and parables of the Prodigal Son (Luke 15), the Woman Caught in Adultery (John 8), and the Rich Young Ruler (Luke 18) the great message of Jesus, exclamation-pointed at the cross, is repentance and forgiveness of sins.

Since the beginning, Jesus' followers have delighted in this incredible gift.

As St. Paul puts it, "He has rescued us from the power of darkness and transferred us into the kingdom of his beloved Son, in whom we have redemption and forgiveness of sins." (Col. 1:13-14) When we repent through Christ all of our failings and shortcomings are amazingly cast aside by a God who loves us uncon-ditionally and unceasingly.

Not that we understand it.

It just is what it is.

Can you believe it?

If you said 'no' you're not alone.

Throughout history Christians have had a huge problem with receiving God's forgiveness. Over and over we ask ourselves: Can God love me that much? Do I deserve this? Can I pay it back?

Yes, no and no.

Our salvation is not based on our generosity, but God's generosity. There's nothing we can do to earn it. There's no way to pay it back. All we can do is treat it like every other gift. Take it, say thanks, enjoy it, and share it.

I think most of us know deep down that our faith is much less about doing—or paying back and it is much more about being—being joyful receivers of this 'amazing' grace.

The problem is never with God, but with us.

Episcopalians and Divorce

A lot of people find their way into the Episcopal Church following a divorce. The Church genu-inely accepts them not be-cause we don't value marriage, but because of the way we understand it. Marriage is a human endeavor and like every-thing else we attempt, we sometimes fail, despite our best efforts. When a marriage fails we believe the first place to help people put their lives back together is at church.

So, the Church rarely requires a formal annulment or a renun-ciation of the previous relation-ship in order to take Communion. Annulments are also not generally required for re-marriage. However we are very concerned that the respon-sibilities arising out of a failed marriage are tended to in appropriate ways.

Divorce is a delicate issue and your local Episcopal clergy would welcome any questions you might have.

"The message of forgiveness says to us, 'Get over yourself!'" writes theologian L. William Countryman, "Get over your goodness and your righteousness, if they threaten to keep you from full participation in your humanity. Get over your faults, your inadequacy, if they're what hold you back. Get over whatever it is that makes you self-obsessed, whatever makes you reject God's wooing of you... whatever makes you imagine that there's something in this world more important and more fundamental than love.

"Instead, be loved.

"Why would you refuse it? Perhaps you do it out of pique because you think God isn't taking you seriously enough. Perhaps you do it out of shame and embarrassment because God is being kinder to you than you think you deserve. Either way, get over yourself. You are forgiven."[2]

This is the Gospel the world is looking for.

It's a lot more appealing to those who are bruised and battered by way too many well-meaning religious people who are morality-obsessed.

In general, Episcopalians don't like to define ourselves by what we're against. We prefer to be known for what we are for. We are for justice, for reconciliation, for forgiveness.

Most of us believe that the Gospel our 15-year-olds need so desperately is not a final exam on the rules of abstinence, sobriety and excess (rules they already know all too well), but assurance that forgiveness is offered to the penitent in Jesus' name.

Let's face it—we know the rules.

And like the stereotypical American tourist trying to order in a Paris café, what we need is not to keep speaking English louder and louder to our francophone waiter, but to try a different language—the language of repentance and forgiveness.

The world of moralism promises a temporary safe haven based on rules we like. Moralism goes fishing through the Bible looking for verses to "prove" a case.

But taking the message of repentance and forgiveness seriously requires a scary step of faith that we'll always be tempted to side step.

Amazing stories
of grace and forgiveness
at
www.theforgivenessproject.com

Ever notice that a lot of the people in the Bible chosen to do God's work led pretty dodgy lives? Take Samson, who just couldn't say "no" to Delilah. Or Jonah, who high-tailed it the other way when God called him to prophesy to Nineveh, and the illustrious St. Paul, whose life goal, at one point, was to pretty much annihilate Christianity.

One danger we get into by preaching moralism versus repentance and forgiveness of sins is that we set up a wall—and one day we may find ourselves on the other side of that wall.

We're all too familiar with the stories of the morals-preaching politician. He gets caught in a seedy hotel room with another woman (or man…)

…Or there's the family values preacher who gets arrested for embezzling from his church.

What they need, what we need, is not to hear more about just how heinous human behavior is—we need the understanding that even our best deeds fall far short of impressing God. We're unable to be revived by 'just following the rules of good behavior.' We're all in dire need of the resurrection hope of Jesus Christ and the promise of God's forgiveness.

Our radical sins need radical forgiveness.

This is what most Episcopalians see as the heart of the Gospel.

We believe God's mercy wins out over God's judgment.

One of the more poignant phrases in our prayer book comes as the priest prays over the bread and wine saying, "yet we beseech thee to accept this our bounden duty and service, not weighing our merits, but pardoning our offences."[3]

While all of us will do plenty of good things in life, most Episcopalians believe God is not a divine Santa Claus—taking note of every good (and bad) deed. God's generosity defies human understandings of who we think are 'naughty and nice.' We rejoice in God's dominant characteristic —to have mercy. We believe God is the supreme expression of love who would much rather forgive than punish.

Yes, Episcopalians take sin seriously.

But we also take forgiveness seriously.

Our prayer book recommends we confess our sins twice a day. Our prayer book recommends we receive God's forgiveness much more often.

This forgiveness is open to all who ask. It's the heart of the Good News: Jesus really means it when He says 'welcome.'

5. ACCEPT

"It is the poetry of faith, not its various dogma,
that persuades us Episcopalians.
The elegance of a doctrine… the music of a holy name…
the cry of an eagle in the chant of a psalm…
These things teach us, though most of them cannot be taught."

Phyllis Tickle

Accept

I remember the first time I set foot inside the largest Gothic building in the United States.

I walked in—and I looked up—and up—and up.

I was at the Episcopal Cathedral of St. John the Divine in New York City.

A volunteer handed me a program. She should've handed me a neck brace.

The awe and grandeur of the place put me in a trance. I spent the afternoon with my neck craned, aimlessly wandering, bouncing off sandstone walls, marble steps and startled children.

Like other cathedrals I'd visited, the sweeping lines of the fan vaulting and the sunlight teeming through the clerestory created an overwhelming sense of majesty. As the afternoon wore on (and my neck got stiffer, though I stopped walking into people), subtle details emerged—the windows, the ceiling, the pillars, the

CATHEDRAL OF ST. JOHN THE DIVINE

St. John the Divine

in New York City (top) is the largest gothic building in the United States. An insert window from the Cathedral shows someone watching television.

carvings, the chapels, and of course, the light. Not only did I know God was there, but I gradually began to feel that God wasn't just there for me—this gargantuan place held room for a lot of people.

There was room for everybody.

I had this overpowering sense of acceptance—that God's arms were wide open. It was most apparent in the stories told in stained glass.

Hundreds of windows represent an amazing variety of people, places, and things. There are the hallowed stand-bys like St. Peter, St. Augustine and Thomas Aquinas. But you also find Martin Luther King, Jr., Albert Einstein, and Gandhi.

You can feel God's acceptance in the chapels as well.

Many of them are dedicated to the ethnic groups of the workers who built the place (which still isn't finished). Other chapels are dedicated to the important things that touch our everyday lives like sports, poetry and AIDS. On the altar you won't just find a cross, but you might also find a menorah or a Shinto vase.

A Jewish visitor once said, "All religions reject, reject, reject, exclude, exclude, exclude, but I come to your Cathedral and what do I find? In statuary and in glass I find labor and management side by side. I find athletics and psychiatry side by side."[1]

And God is right in the middle of it all.

One of the more scandalous aspects of Jesus' ministry is that he kept hanging around people others had rejected. Religious people made fun of Jesus for having dinner with prostitutes and tax collectors. They mocked him for turning simple fishermen into theologians. They just didn't understand how any self-respecting rabbi would let so many women hang out with him. Jesus made it pretty clear that his job wasn't to impress powerful people. His job was to make friends with the people who had no friends.

His job was not to reject, but to accept. In tens of thousands of pieces of stained glass of every size and rainbow color, inside a surplus of chapels, housed inside one of the biggest places human hands can make, is a tangible representation of this incredible decree.

St. John the Divine is a grand testament to something even grander:

In God's house, there's a place for everybody.

Via Media

This radical notion of inclusion that always strikes me at St. John's is something Episcopalians inherited quite a while ago.

It's a long story with a colorful cast of characters and a delicious array of plots. Movies about it win Oscars.

As you may know, the Episcopal Church is a direct descendant of the Church of England.

It was formed in the early 1500's after King Henry VIII and Parliament said they no longer wanted the Pope ruling England's churches—or taking its money. The newly formed Church of England didn't change its worship or theology. Henry wasn't out to create a new institution or break with Rome. He simply wanted more control.

But as the Protestants on the European continent gained power, the English church came under increasing pressure to change what it believed.

When Henry VIII died his young son Edward VI took the Church in a Protestant direction. His untimely death (pneumonia) a few years later put his sister Mary Tudor on the throne. She was a devout Roman Catholic and began moving the Church back toward Rome.

During both Edward and Mary's short reigns hundreds of people were killed in the name of religion.

Protestants killed Catholics. Catholics killed Protestants.
That's how Mary earned the nickname 'Bloody Mary.'

Like Edward, she also died young (stomach cancer), leaving the throne to her sister Elizabeth.

Elizabeth I, more than anybody else, gave our faith its distinctive shape, especially its bent towards tolerance and acceptance.

When Elizabeth took the throne, England was a mess. Religious unrest, fear, and confusion reigned. Faced with warring Protestants and Catholics she knew she had to find a compromise, a middle way. Elizabeth wanted all English Christians to feel welcome at their church. Her solution wasn't a Church of Geneva (Protestant) or a Church of Rome (Catholic)—but something unique in more than just name—the Church of England.

Elizabeth saw to it that much of traditional Roman Catholic faith and practice stuck around—though still, no Pope. She also sympathized with Protestants by making sure English language Bibles were available in parishes. While she preferred a celibate clergy, she allowed priests and bishops to get married, something that had been widely accepted for the first thousand years of Christianity anyway.

While Elizabeth made church membership mandatory, she also gave lots of latitude to individual conscience. She famously told Parliament, "The Church shall not build windows into men's souls."

Elizabeth sat on the throne for 45 years. She brought stability to England. And in the process she made the Church of England a place where Christians with different points of view could find a home.

Elizabeth I

Known as the Virgin Queen, Elizabeth probably had more effect on the shape of the Anglican faith (and, hence, the Episcopal Church) than anybody else, including her father, King Henry VIII. The films Elizabeth I and Elizabeth: The Golden Age with Cate Blanchett are highly recommended.

This via media (Latin for 'middle way') remains a defining characteristic of my Church.

While some people say we're indecisive and lukewarm, our inclusiveness and acceptance is something we really value. Most of us see compromise and negotiation as a way to practice Christian charity. We also see it as vital to the work of advancing the Gospel.

Few among us have not learned that truth rarely lies in the extreme, but is usually found somewhere in the middle.

Tutu

Sometimes it pays to get to work early.

Which is rare for me, but is exactly what happened on that unforgettable August morning when a colleague knocked on my door.

She was holding a black case that we use to take communion on the road, usually for sick people and prison inmates. She asked if I would join her. I said sure.
And I wondered who was ill or who'd been locked up overnight.

She said we're going to celebrate communion with Archbishop Desmond Tutu of South Africa.

And no, she assured me, he was not on his deathbed or in the clink.

Tutu is the 1984 Nobel Peace Prize laureate. He was in town for a conference, and for the next four days my colleague and I had the magical experience of beginning each morning with him. There, in that modest hotel suite, we gathered around a small dining room table and celebrated a simple Eucharist. Here we saw first-hand the spiritual practices of a respected Christian and world-class peacemaker.

Archbishop Tutu is bubbly, energetic, intelligent, and very funny (auto-graphing a book for my dad, "Dear Father—you have good genes"). But what is most memorable is his humble devotion to the Christian life. During our liturgy he prayed earnestly for people suffering from war, famine and disease. He spoke passionately about the Christian responsi-bility to bring justice and compassion to the world, which is something he knows a thing or two about because he has spent most of his life at the forefront of this fight for justice.

If you think about all the revolutions the world witnessed in the late 20th century (the fall of the Berlin Wall, the opening of Eastern Bloc countries), the ending of apartheid in South Africa was one of the most dramatic.

Years of turmoil and violence prefaced the events that finally allowed the majority black population to share power with the white government. Tutu was right in the thick of this action as a national and international spokesman and as a spiritual leader. He won the Nobel Prize for his role, and created a new model of Christian leadership.

Following the change in government it became apparent that the gross violations of human rights committed over the years were simply too egregious to overlook. Massacres, rapes, thievery, and sordidness of all kinds plagued the country between 1960 and 1994.

Deep wounds persisted.
Retribution reigned.
Peace hung by a thread.

In 1995, when apartheid had ended, the South African government passed a bill creating the Truth and Reconciliation Commission. Tutu was a staunch supporter. The aim was to heal a broken country that might not otherwise have survived. Victims of injustice sent in thousands of requests for hearings. The Commission held public meetings across the country to hear from victims and violators alike and to help them make amends. The meetings were much cheaper than taking every suspect to court—many crimes had no living witnesses.

South African President Nelson Mandela chose Archbishop Tutu to lead the Commission. Tutu knew a middle way had to be found.

"Often in South Africa, you heard people say, 'Let bygones be bygones.' And you say, unfortunately, they don't become bygones just because, by fiat, you declare them to be so..."

The solution meant amnesty for confessors, and an opportunity for these violators to face victims, "We need to do all we can to help our children appropriate their history, appropriate their memory."[2]

The stories of peacemaking that came out of these hearings bring tears to my eyes (actually, I'm not alone, it was nicknamed 'the Kleenex Commission). Murderers were shaking hands with victim's families. Women who were raped were making peace with their assailants. Robbery victims were hugging the thugs who had ransacked their houses.

Because of the Archbishop's work, thousands of children now have very different memories of this violent transition. Hope and confidence have been rekindled.

It's not enough to want peace.
You've got to work for it.
You've got to find a middle way.

This is something Archbishop Tutu is still trying to do. He has his hands in all kinds of projects. One of them is with my church. The Desmond Tutu Education Center at General Seminary in New York is a start. It's a place where people share ideas about peacemaking and finding a middle way. It serves seminarians and visitors from around the world by offering classes, guest speakers, meeting places, books and other literature. The idea is to get people talking about peace.

This is a great idea.

Think about all the resources we spend making war.

Think about the guns and tanks and M.R.E.s and fighter planes and battleships and Kevlar… and people.

Then think about how much we spend waging peace.

How invested are we in finding ways to avoid confrontation?

How much do we really care about finding creative ways to overcome our differences? How seriously do we take Jesus' life and teachings, which were based on peace and reconciliation? How hard are we looking for a via media?

The world is getting smaller.
War is getting easier.

Arguments that once ended in standoffs are escalating into terrifying acts of violence. Yesterday's name callers and rock throwers are today's hijackers and suicide bombers.

We have to find ways to bridge our differences without fighting.

Finding a Middle Way

BEYER BLINDER BELLE, LLP

The Desmond Tutu Education Center at General Seminary in New York City is devoted to finding new ways to make peace. It houses programs like the new Center for Peace and Reconciliation and the Center for Jewish-Christian Studies and Relations. Tutu is a member of the Anglican Church of South Africa, a sister church to the Episcopal Church.

We have to find ways to solve our problems without killing ourselves. We have to find ways to wage peace. Violence no longer threatens unstable countries in faraway places. We all know that we are all at risk.

It's life or death, like never before.

I am so thankful for every person on the face of the planet who is trying to find a middle way. I thank God for people who make the decision every day to suffer humiliation by not hitting back. I applaud everybody who's made it their life's quest to dispel aggression and turn the other cheek. This is the kind of work God wants us to do. Peacemakers are the kinds of people God wants us to be.

And we desperately need churches that will inspire us to do that.

We need churches that will never stop telling us that icy stand-offs and swift retributions are not our only options.

Danforth

You've got to wonder how John Danforth ever made it through cocktail parties.

How do you avoid talking about religion and politics when you're an Episcopal priest and a U.S. Senator?

It could be because he has had practice.

Ever since college, Danforth has balanced two very different callings. When he went to graduate school he attended law school and divinity school at the same time. During his three terms in the Senate, work in Africa and at the U.N., Danforth managed to moonlight at a D.C. parish.

Reconciliation

Author of: Faith and Politics: How the Moral Values Debate Divides America and How to Move Forward Together.

The two callings convinced him of one thing—the absolutely essential role of reconciliation in accomplishing anything of lasting value.

"I believe that the central message of the Episcopal Church and of all Christians," says Danforth, "is and should be that God was in Christ reconciling the world to himself and that he has entrusted to us the ministry of reconciliation."[3] Danforth's vision for Christianity is to see us get more involved in helping people get along. There are all kinds of opportunities for reconciliation in the world just waiting to be taken on. All kinds of opportunities for reconciliation are just waiting for churches to take on.

Not long ago the head of the U.N. wrote a report to the General Assembly on terrorism. It recommended a highly visible, constructive dialogue between members of different religions. Danforth says this is where churches should be —right in the thick of helping the world make peace. "We could help form an interfaith mediation service to address very practical questions of the religious element of conflict, such as the application of Sharia law in Khartoum; that kind of thing. We could do that."

Danforth, and others like him, who are persistently reminding us of our meta-roles as reconcilers and peacemakers, are crucial voices for us today.

Jesus doesn't just call us to make peace within our families. Jesus calls us to make peace with our community, our nation and with our world.

I think that's what Jesus meant when he called us, 'a light to the world.'

The Book of Revelation puts it like this.
It paints a picture of heaven as 'the New Jerusalem.' It is a city.
It is not an empty field. It is not a gated community. It is an open market.
It is a place where everybody lives together in one place—in peace. It is a place where arguments, fistfights and world wars have ceased. It is a place where we all finally get along.

How do we get ourselves ready to live in a place like that? How do we help our neighbors, our country and our world live in that place? How do we make that place, this place?

I'm convinced that the hard road to heaven is a middle road.

This has always been a distinctive message of my church.

We have always seen ourselves as a via media—the middle way. We have always seen ourselves as a place where people from many different places with many different points of view can come together around one altar.

Around Christ's altar there's a place for everybody.

6. THANK

We don't gather around the Communion Table
to escape the world's problems, but to escape the world's answers.

Bishop Arthur Vogel

Thank

Every night at 7:30 a group of about twenty men shuffles into the basement of our local homeless shelter and finds a spot in the handful of dingy old church pews set up in the chapel.

It's time for the evening service.

Most of them are tired, haggard and hungry—for more than just food. Most of them are looking for direction, forgiveness, hope and love.
A few are looking for another bottle, a fix, or a quiet place to crash.

But for a variety of reasons, this is where they come.

Dan, Linda, and I are among the many ministers who regularly hold services here. For most of these men, it's the first time they've ever met an Episcopalian. Homeless shelters are a United Nations of religion and Episcopalians are from a very small country.

So we happily explain how we do Christianity. One of the first things we ask is, "How many of you have ever gone over to your grandmother's house on Thanksgiving?" Everybody raises their hand. "What does the dinner table look like? Are there styrofoam plates? Plastic forks? Do you wear a dirty t-shirt and cut off shorts? Does somebody walk in late with a bag of cold burgers and yell 'dig in?'"

Of course not.

They begin to tell me about their family's special traditions, where Grandma's china came from, who carves the turkey, and why that old lace tablecloth is only used once a year.

Meanwhile, Dan meticulously sets the communion table.
Linda chooses the hymns.
And we all talk about the nuts and bolts of reverence, ceremony and prayer. It breaks the ice for the practice of the ancient and sacred tradition before us. It's a holy ritual that will help us see Jesus in an authentic and awesome way. It will help us do what every one of us is here to do.

We've come to say thanks.

The Bible tells us that on the night before Jesus died, he took bread and wine. He thanked God for it. He blessed it, broke it, and gave it to his disciples. Ever since this 'last supper,' God's Church has been doing its best to imitate this sublime act. Through the years and among different church groups, the ceremony has taken on different shapes as people of faith respond to the call to worship. My church has its own take. It's certainly not the only one. It might not be the best one. But it's worked for millions of us, for a long time.

Episcopalians like to think of every Sunday as Thanksgiving Day.

As I've mentioned, the word Eucharist is an ancient Greek word that means 'thanksgiving' (it's almost the identical word you hear in Greece today when people say 'thank you').

When we come together on Sundays we want to give thanks well.

Many of us (clergy especially) take great care in the way we dress for this rite. We try to hire the best musicians and preachers. We carefully decorate our church and set the Communion table. We often march around in formal processions when we come in and go out. We're well aware that our most honored guest is Jesus Christ who said, "Where two or three are gathered in my name, I am there among them." (Matt. 18:20).

It's a daunting notion to suppose that the Creator of the Universe, the King of Kings and Lord of Lords—the owner of the cattle of a thousand hills—actually meets us.

That's why we take such care.

That's why we put so much thought and energy into our thoughts and words. We believe Sunday worship is our most profound corporate response to Christ's grace and presence among us.

Most Episcopalians believe that our worship services should reflect reverence in beauty and ritual to best express our gratitude to God. Christians understand worship to be honor directed to God through Jesus Christ.

Within the Church this 'work' of worship is called liturgy, which comes from another Greek word literally meaning 'work of the people.'

Every church has a liturgy, no matter how laid back or informal - if people are getting together to worship, it's liturgy. It's a 'work of the people.'

Like all other Christians, Episcopalians have a distinctive way of sorting out the how, when, why, and where of worship. Like other Christians, our tradition has been passed down for centuries, refined, shaped, and honed in distinctive ways that we've come to cherish.

Episcopalians see their call to worship rooted in the words of Jesus when he said, "'you shall love the Lord your God with all your heart, and with all your soul, and with all your mind.' This is the greatest and first commandment." (Matt. 22:37)

When we come together on Sundays, we're responding to this call.
We're acknowledging the love given to us, and offering our love in return.

Most Episcopalians operate from this fundamental, biblical conviction that the Church's primary goal is to worship God—to say thanks.

More Than a Feeling

One Sunday morning, following services, a bishop I know was standing by the back door of the church greeting parishioners as they left.

A young man stopped to shake hands

He said, "Bishop, I really didn't like that last hymn."

The cheeky bishop smiled and said, "That's OK, we didn't sing it for you." One of the most significant trends we're witnessing today is this growing sense of cultural and personal narcissism. Many of us see it in the Church. Subtly but increasingly, many people no longer come to church to give, but to get. In Christian circles I've heard people talk about whether or not they were "fed" at church. This is a harmless enough comment, but it betrays a self-centeredness that seems to miss the whole point of going to church. As the bishop might explain, we don't come together on Sundays primarily to please ourselves, but to worship God.

Now this doesn't mean that we should choose our churches by finding boring ones (we may discover a depressingly wide selection). However, it is to point out that we all have a tendency to let our own individualism adversely affect our church-going decisions.

I worry that not enough of us realize this.

Wade Clark Roof has done significant research into why baby boomers, in particular, tend to behave this way. Many boomers, who left church when they were younger, are now coming back. But Roof says they're using culturally influenced criteria, based on personal 'choices' and 'needs' to choose their worshipping communities.[1] An individualized sense of 'feeling' is replacing the older, more communitarian framework held by past generations. This puts tremendous pressure on churches to change what they do, not out of theological conviction, but because that's how we can attract more people.

Nearly every church I know is under this kind of pressure.

Like other Christian communities, most Episcopalians have been hesitant to change the way we worship based on the latest trends. It's not simply because we're sentimental, it's because we're cautious. As one Lutheran theologian famously warned, "to give the whole store away to match what this year's market says the unchurched want is to have the people who know least about the faith determine most about its expression."[2]

As a preacher, the highest compliment I can get is not, 'oh you brought me to tears,' or 'I feel so uplifted now,' but 'you really made me think.' I hope that a sermon gives people something to chew on all week, something they just can't figure out by the end of the service.

Most Episcopalians believe sermons need to be about more than motivational speaking, cheerleading and pop psychology. Sure, they should appeal to our hearts, but they also need to make a serious attempt to appeal to our minds.

When we select music for our services we really do care about how people feel when they sing. We want our music to be uplifting and inspiring. However we tend to avoid filling it with the kind of lyrics that might lead us to believe that our singing is all about us.

Because it's not. It's all about God.

Episcopalians tend to be drawn to music that exhibits a more formal beauty, eloquence and imagination in text and tune. We don't like to think of ourselves as dedicated to our hymns out of a banal sense of romanticism. Rather, we cherish our music because much of it has been tried (many times, for centuries) and found to be the most fitting, theologically and musically, to worship the Holy One who is at the center of our worship.

Bach, Handel, Wesley and Watts have produced some of the most incredible music the world has ever heard. This is not to say that Episcopalians only sing old songs. There are plenty of contemporary musicians who are making significant contributions to the church.

The reason we're so taken by this particular repertoire is because, in a very profound sense, it speaks of our longing to offer our best—our very best—for God's glory.

We want to give thanks well.

This is not to pass judgment on the worship practices of others or to say that our way is the only way. Rather it is to point out that Episcopalians give great thought and effort into every aspect of our worship.

Episcopalians & the Arts

Traditionally, Episcopalians have been keen supporters of the arts. Many parishes host art exhibits, concerts and welcome liturgical dancing.

Like many churches, we understand that the greatest art ever created has been done in celebration of the spiritual. This is a tradition we believe helps us become better Christians. Researcher Robert Wuthnow has found, "people with greater exposure to artistic activities are more likely than those with less exposure to be seriously committed to spiritual growth."[3]

Most Episcopalians strive for excellence in worship because it says something very important about how we see and respond to God. "When [Episcopalianism] is at its best, its liturgy, its poetry, its music and its life can create a world of wonder in which it is very easy to fall in love with God."[3]

Space

Given these convictions it's not hard to figure out why the architecture and furnishings of our buildings look the way they do.

Notice the basic shape of many of our churches. They're cross-shaped. Many of them are designed so that the congregation faces east. This reflects a traditional belief that Christ will return from that direction. We want to be reminded that Christ is coming again.

Inside the church, the altar is usually the first thing to catch our eye. Although some churches have huge pulpits and baptismal fonts, it's the altar that usually takes center stage. For most of us its centrality tells us that the Eucharist is at the heart of what brings us together.

Artwork adorns many of our churches, especially stained glass. Its origins date back to a time when illiteracy was rampant and the Christian story was best told with pictures (they have also served as convenient alternatives to boring sermons, though this has never happened at my church...). Other common furnishings include the Stations of the Cross (pictures or plaques of the events of Jesus' last hours) and colorful banners to remind us of the Christian seasons.

Like a lot of faith traditions, Episcopalians like to name their churches after Christians who have led ex-

---

Cracking the Color Code

Color is a strong symbol for Episcopalians. Early on, Christians designated certain colors to mark the seasons.

They remind us of Christ's life and work.

Advent (4 weeks before Christmas)
  Purple/Blue Preparation/Expectation
Christmas
  White Celebration/Incarnation
Epiphany (January 6)
  Green Revealing
Lent (winter)
  Purple Penance/Inner Reflection
Holy Week (spring)
  Blood Red
  Commemoration/Sacrifice
Easter (spring)
  White Celebration/Victory
Pentecost (early summer)
  Red Holy Spirit Given to All
Season after Pentecost (summer)
  Green Spirit leads/teaches. Growth

---

emplary lives—saints. St. John is the most common saint found in Episcopal Church names. We also name churches after events and church seasons like Epiphany, Advent, and the Transfiguration. Christ Church is the most common name of all for Episcopal Churches. We believe that the worship environment, down to its very name, has no small effect on the formation of our communities and our souls.

Most of us choose to worship in places that look and sound holy because deep in our hearts we want to be holy. The word holy simply means set apart. Christians are called to be set apart for God's purposes.

Not the world's purposes. God's purposes.

A large trend in church architecture today is to downplay the traditional aspects of worship spaces in favor of a more homogenous, non-offensive design. Episcopalians are generally hesitant to follow this trend. We tend to value our traditional architecture not only because we value tradition, but also because we recognize the impact of aesthetic on our souls. As Winston Churchill put it, humans shape buildings, then our buildings shape us. Indeed, we are children of our environment.

Eucharist

Not long ago a group of sociologists published a fascinating study on loneliness. Researchers interviewed hundreds of people and reported that one-fourth of all Americans say they had nobody to talk to about "important matters." Another one-fourth said they were only one person away from having nobody to talk to. However, what was most disconcerting was that an identical study was completed two decades before.

And in just twenty years researchers found the number of people with no one to confide in had doubled.[4]

For a lot of reasons, we're not connecting with one another like we used to. We're not widening our circles of close friends. We're drawing these circles in. Not only are we failing to maintain our relationships, we're also failing to reach out and establish friendships with people we don't know.

We need communion.

It's a spiritual and a physical yearning. Researchers say social isolation is as big a risk factor for premature death as smoking. Isolation adds to social problems, like racial tensions. It robs us of differing viewpoints and adds to the polarization of our societies.

While Christians are certainly not immune to this trend, we do offer a solution. Communion—aka—Eucharist.

In that small act of sharing a meal, Jesus gave the Church a huge gift.

Through time this simple act has served as a literal and symbolic focal point to bring everybody together, regardless of income, race, age, citizenship, marital status or gender preference.

The Eucharist is the great equalizer.

In an age when communal touchstones are scarce, the Eucharist provides us with an unparalleled centerpiece.

Eucharist. It's about more than Jesus' life. It's about our lives. Jesus' body was broken and his blood was poured out so that our lives would be better. We're the beneficiaries of a stranger's sacrifice.

And we're not supposed to simply take Eucharist. We're supposed to be Eucharist. In this communal meal we too pour ourselves out for the world. We too see strangers become the beneficiaries of our sacrifices. We too see that in our humble attempts to imitate Christ, we begin to heal our shattered world. One person at a time. One relationship at a time. We're brought together, not apart, by Eucharist.

That's a big reason why Christians have always placed such a high value on his Holy Communion. St. Paul, who wrote the earliest New Testament books, said we should share Eucharist all the time, "For as often as you eat this bread and drink the cup, you proclaim the Lord's death until he comes." (1 Cor. 11:23-26)

That's what the first Christians did.

They were Jews, so their practice evolved from what they already knew. They continued to meet weekly, but they changed the day. They deliberately met on Sunday, which was the day of Jesus' resurrection instead of Saturday, the Jewish Sabbath day. At first they broke bread and offered prayers, as was the Jewish custom. But following Christ's appearance, they understood the meaning of their last supper together and created a

U2CHARIST

A worship service to end poverty, hunger and AIDS around the globe. Through spoken word, prayer and the music of U2, we'll explore how we can make a lasting difference in our world.

St. David's Episcopal Church

Episcopal worship isn't limited to specific musical genres. New forms, like Jazz masses, Taize, Celtic and even the U2charist found in some parishes. They help us form community in authentic, and creative ways.

new ritual (practice) as directed by Christ. The new ritual went by several names, 'the Lord's Supper,' 'the breaking of the bread,' 'the love feast,' 'the memorial' and Communion. As the Church evolved, the theology and ceremony grew more and more complex. By the fourth century, people were calling the ritual the Eucharist, 'the mystery' or 'the sacrament.'[5]

A second century prayer reflects the unity we still cherish as a part of this holy meal, "As this broken bread was scattered upon the mountains, but was brought together and made one, so let your church be gathered together from the ends of the earth into your kingdom."[6]

Mystery

So what exactly happens at the Eucharist? Do the bread and wine literally become Christ's body and blood? Or are they symbols of a larger mystery?

Through the years Christians have explained this in a million different ways. Roman Catholics are known for something called Transubstantiation. Lutherans have promoted Consubstantiation. And Baptists have embraced Memorialism, just to name a few.

Episcopalians, in our tendency to seek a middle way, hold to something called Real Presence. It means we really believe Christ is present in the Eucharist though we're deliberately hesitant to try to explain it. One theologian explains, "Christ's presence is objectively and spiritually real, not merely a psychological experience. Rather it is a sacramen-

---

Episcopalians and Sacraments

Episcopalians recognize certain acts as 'sacraments.' This word means, "an outward and visible sign of an inward and spiritual grace." For example, Baptism is a Sacrament. The outward and visible sign is water and the inward and spiritual grace is the washing away of sin.

Episcopalians recognize two great sacraments as those handed down by Jesus; Baptism and Holy Communion.

However, we also recognize five lesser sacraments; Marriage, Reconciliation of the Penitent (also called 'Confession'), Ordination, Ministration to the Sick and Dying (also called 'last rites') and Confirmation (including Reception into the Church and the Reaffirmation of Baptismal Vows).

tal presence, different from the manner which physical objects are present, yet nonetheless real."[7]

This belief was honed for us back in the 16th and 17th centuries during Elizabeth's reign. As you may remember, Elizabeth was faced with a volatile religious atmosphere and was trying to make peace between warring Protestants and Catholics. One of the more contentious issues was the meaning of the Eucharist. In general terms, Catholics had a more literal view of Christ's presence while Protestants held to a more symbolic view. After hearing arguments from both sides Elizabeth and her religious thinkers decided on a compromise. They proposed a middle way, crediting Elizabeth with the authorship of this simple poem:

> Christ was the Word that spake it;
> He took the bread and break it;
> Whatever God doth make it,
> I do believe and take it.

When we try to explain the Eucharist we soon find our arguments taking us in circles.

And people haven't just argued over this concept. They've killed over it. Your opinion on this simple act was a matter of life and death.

Elizabeth knew this.

When we talk about the Eucharist we get on a train bound for mystery. Our only difference is on which stop we get off. So instead of concentrating on something we can never solve (much less agree on), we're better off concentrating on something more productive—like how the Eucharist is affecting us and our community. One theologian says, "The Anglican reformers… were not concerned so much with the transformation of the bread and wine on the altar as they were with the transformation of the lives of Christian people."[8] Instead of endlessly debating how exactly Jesus comes into the communion elements, let's ask how Jesus is coming into you and me.

How does Eucharist change us?

How does Eucharist shape us?

How does Eucharist help us change the world?

Like most Christians, Episcopalians approach the Communion table with awe, reverence and humility, admitting that we don't have it all figured out. We come to hold Jesus to the promise that he's here, somehow and some way, to meet us, comfort us, heal us, assure us, and save us.

The Eucharist is our weekly altar call.

This is the most profound opportunity for each of us to accept Jesus anew into our hearts, to be transformed and 'born again' in the truest sense of the words.

Episcopalians know we are not the only ones called to Christ's table. That's why we open our table to everybody.

Christ's altar is not our own.

It's God's.

All baptized Christians, Catholics, Lutherans, Baptists, Pentecostal, Wesleyan, etc., regardless of Christian heritage, are welcome to receive the bread and wine at Episcopal services.

All others are invited to come forward as well and receive a blessing from the minister. Episcopalians see the Communion table as just that—a table at which all Christians may commune.

Christian unity based on Christ.

That's why the high point of our monthly visits to the homeless shelter is the Eucharist. Circled around that rickety old, card table. We represent a wide swath of Christ's church and hold an equally wide variety of beliefs.

We hold hands. We close our eyes. And we pray the Our Father. The bread is broken. The fruit of the vine is poured. And we know that Christ's body and blood has trumped our differences.

Our relationship with Christ has been made new—amidst friendships that are equally new.

As we turn to go, we share hugs and smiles and most every night, the atmosphere is more hope-filled than when we began.

For Christ has been with us.

And we've said thanks.

7. SHAPE

"You do not think your way into a new way of living,
you live your way into a new way of thinking."

Koininia Community

Shape

I remember reading an interesting historical study on the diaries of teenage girls.[1] Its authors began by studying the private journals of young women from the late 1800's.

Most of these diaries had been kept hidden under lock and key. The entries showed these young ladies had incredible maturity and poise. They wrote passionately and intelligently about their main goals in life—self-control, charity, and building character based on service to others. They showed a sobriety and self-confidence, which the girls saw as integral to living productive and virtuous lives. They were obviously shaped by the dominant Victorian strains of their era.

Researchers then hit fast forward and compared these journals with the diaries of today's teens.

Of course they didn't need keys to open them.
They were posted on the Internet.
When you read them, there's no question these are also coming from young minds deeply shaped by their culture.

The average teenage girl is exposed to three thousand commercial images a day.[2] These images tout glamour, glitz and all the allure of the latest trinkets and fashions.

They promote images of unrealistic body types—the average young woman on the cover of a beauty magazine is 5 feet 11 inches and weighs 110 pounds. These measurements represent only 3% of the female population. The incredible influence of these images comes out in these diaries. One sociologist described them as little more than, "catalogs of desires for improved body features and plans for their pursuit."

There's no question that our culture shapes us. It influences us to embrace specific ideals based on specific values. It shapes our desires, goals and the way we understand our deepest selves.

Jesus offers to shape us in another way. It's very different than the way the world shapes us. Jesus wants to shape us in ways that give us the true meaning we all yearn for—and will help us shape our culture, in turn, for the better.

This is one big reason Christians establish churches—we're not just talking buildings, but communities of people with shared convictions. We come together not only to worship, but also to become places that reinforce our shared Christian values of love, hope, compassion, inclusion and hospitality.

Episcopalians see the formation and nurturing of community as one of our most important callings. Like many churches, we see our task of shaping people as a way we live out Jesus' words to, "go therefore and make disciples of all nations" (Matt. 28:19). Liturgy is one of the primary ways the Church builds community and forms disciples.

Liturgy

One thing I really love about my job is leading the Eucharistic prayer (the prayer over the bread and wine) at Sunday morning worship services.

My arms are spread wide as I stand behind the altar facing everybody and praying the familiar words that I read from a big red book. When I look out at the congregation I see most people intently listening (at least this is what I like to think they're doing).

Some people are standing. Some people are kneeling.
Though only one person is actually mouthing the words back to me.
Her name is Adrian. She has this long prayer memorized.

She's nine years old.

Adrian was baptized at my church. She has grown up attending Sunday school. She's an acolyte and a member of the children's choir. She rarely misses church. She's known the words of the Eucharistic prayer for years. She also knows the Nicene Creed, a fair share of the hymns and the Post Communion prayer. There's no question that the liturgy has had a profound affect on her life. If her father and grandfather, who were raised in much the same way, are any indication, Adrian is destined to be one of the most devout Christians I'll ever know.

She already is.

Liturgy does this to people. Young and old. Liturgy has the ability to shape us in ways we know and ways we'll never know.

It is the magic of this amazing story of sacrifice, forgiveness and love repeated in the Church's words and actions week after week that has an immeasurable effect on us. As one theologian says, churches are fundamentally communities of memory, "where the old stories are retold, and where the retelling is accompanied with the sights, sounds and smells that embed them in subterranean levels of consciousness."[3]

That's one reason most of our churches encourage kids to participate. We welcome kids as acolytes, choristers, readers, and ushers—anywhere we can put them. We know the cumulative effect of the liturgy on lives big and small.

The book of Proverbs says, 'Raise up a child in the way that he (or she) should go, and when they are old, they shall not depart from it.'

Liturgy helps us raise kids who know their identities are not based on how they look or what they own. Liturgy helps us raise kids who know their identities are not based on who the world says they are. Liturgy helps us raise kids whose identities are deeply shaped by the story of Jesus.

Family

A child's first experience in an Episcopal church is one they usually don't remember. Episcopalians baptize babies. (more on page 155).

That means we bring together parents, grandparents, friends and the congregation to celebrate and witness this pinnacle event in a Christian's life.

Although the parish may play a crucial role in the child's growth and development, just as important is our responsibility to help parents. Helping parents be parents. Raising a child takes more than two people. It takes a much bigger family.

Shaping Our Kids

Keeping kids in church is a major challenge today. Many parishes are effectively meeting it with some dynamic and effective curriculums.

Some of the more popular programs have been developed by Morehouse Publishing, (All Things New, Episcopal Children's Curriculum) and LeaderResources (Journey to Adulthood). Check them out at:

www.morehousepublishing.org

www.leaderresources.org

One of my favorite Sunday school teachers is Noreen. She has kids. She has grandkids. But she doesn't have any of them in her Sunday school class. Instead, she has a dozen rambunctious teenagers who have no blood relation to her whatsoever.

So why do they call her "Mom?" It's because Noreen is family.

It's in the selfless ways she gives of herself, week after week, lesson after lesson, pizza night after pizza night, mission trip after mission trip. Noreen, like the millions of other Sunday school teachers around the world, shows our kids in the most profound ways, that they're important, accepted, and most of all, that they're loved.

Many Episcopal churches offer some pretty dynamic curriculums to help us raise our kids. The best ones reflect our commitment to reason and an age-appropriate attentiveness to depth and rigor. We know that too much youth ministry takes place in the shallow end of the theological pool.

So many of our parishes are committed to curriculums like 'Catechesis of the Good Shepherd,' 'Godly Play' and 'Worship Center,' which are based on Montessori principles. 'Journey to Adulthood' provides relational, small group settings for junior high and high school aged kids. They offer strong liturgical components. They culminate in mission trips and pilgrimages that are often life changing.

Once kids turn 16 many parishes encourage them to serve as leaders on the Vestry (our church board). Teens are also eligible to take leadership roles on diocesan, even national church boards.

We like to think that our children are not the future of the Episcopal Church.

Our children are the Episcopal Church.

Becoming Adult

Despite the profound affect our liturgy can have on us as adults, we realize that many of us only spend an hour or two a week in church.

That's if we go every week. That's out of 168 hours in a week.

We need more than that.

As we touched on in Chapter Two, many Americans suffer from religious

Episcopal Schools and Colleges

NOAH SHELDON

There are hundreds of Episcopal pre-school, elementary, and high schools in the U. S. Here's a list of colleges, including Bard College home of the Frank Gehry designed Performing Arts Center (above):

- Bard College, Annandale-on-Hudson, NY

- Clarkson College, Omaha, NE

- Hobart/William Smith Colleges, Geneva, NY

- Kenyon College, Gambier, OH

- St. Augustine College, Chicago, IL

- St. Augustine's College, Raleigh, NC

- St. Paul's College, Lawrenceville, VA

- The University of the South, Sewanee, TN

- Voorhees College, Denmark, SC

illiteracy. Pollster George Gallup, Jr. says we generally operate on a primary school faith level. His polls tell us Americans, "don't know what they believe or why." He says most of us don't know who preached the Sermon on the Mount (it was Jesus, but you knew that).[4]

This seems odd when we consider that many of us continue to take college classes throughout our lives. Many of us continue to exercise and eat right throughout our lives. But why don't we continue to pursue with the same vigor the development of what we say is the most important aspect of our lives —our spirituality? This is a challenge for most every Christian and every congregation, including mine— although we do have some important things to offer.

Adult education in most Episcopal churches often reflects our convictions of listening and open-mindedness. Following the events of September 11, 2001 some churches reacted with pro-military sermons and pledges of government support. Others, including many Episcopal congregations, reacted differently—by offering forums explaining Islam and promoting dialog between Christians and Muslims.

In fact, guest speaker forums are a staple at many Episcopal parishes. Many of us believe that part of the church's mission is to provide conversation places for divergent points of view. Episcopal churches typically welcome 12-step programs to use their facilities. It's also common to find book clubs and short classes in various Christian formation topics.

For years, the University of the South at Sewanee, Tennessee has offered a course called Education for Ministry (E.F.M.) through local parishes. This four-year curriculum is designed for lay people and approaches the rigor of seminary training. Students study the Old and New Testaments, church history, liturgy and theology. They meet regularly, usually once a week in seminars under the guidance of trained and certified mentors. (www. sewanee.edu/EFM/index.htm).

In fact, Episcopal seminaries are rich resources for continuing education. Many offer courses during the year and over the summer. Most are open to the public. The Church Divinity School of the Pacific offers dozens of graduate-level courses online. (Center for Anglican Learning and Leadership www.cdsp.edu/center.php). These are also affordable, with discounts offered if you sign up with friends.

Episcopal Seminaries

While these graduate schools mainly educate candidates for ordained ministry, most also welcome lay people who are interested in growing in Christian knowledge.

- Berkeley Divinity School at Yale, New Haven, CT
- Bexley Hall, Colgate-Rochester,
- Columbus, OH
- Church Divinity School of the Pacific, Berkeley, CA
- Episcopal Divinity School, Cambridge, MA
- Episcopal Theological Seminary of the Southwest, Austin, TX
- General Theological Seminary, New York, NY
- Nashotah House, Nashotah, WI
- Seabury-Western Seminary, Chicago, IL
- Sewanee, University of the South, Sewanee, TN
- Trinity Episcopal School for Ministry, Ambridge, PA
- Virginia Theological Seminary, Alexandria, VA

Money

But when it comes to shaping our lives, few things have the huge influence on North Americans that money does.

It shapes us more than we like to admit.

It shaped the teachings of Jesus who talked more about money than anything else (besides the Kingdom of God).

One of the debts I owe to my church is that it has helped me talk about my own money issues, even though the conversation is an ongoing and difficult one. Maybe it's because we North Americans are so darn rich. And the Bible doesn't speak too highly about rich people.

Even the most cursory reading of the Gospels casts a shadow upon the well to do. Jesus says in Matthew 19:23 "Truly I tell you, it will be hard for a rich person to enter the kingdom of heaven." The famous prayer of praise of Jesus' mother, Mary in Luke 1:53 says, "He has filled the hungry with good things, and sent the rich away empty." And in Luke 6:24 Jesus says, "Woe to you who are rich, for you have received your consolation." The list goes on.

Sure, we may not feel rich. But we make up 5% of the world's population and use about 30% of its resources. We spend more money at Starbucks some mornings than most people make in a day. We live in the richest, most affluent and well-armed nation the world has ever known. And while much of the world goes to bed hungry, we go to bed guilty.

Influenced by what marketers call the 'ad-cult' of buy-now-pay-later, most of us are mercilessly sucked into the acquisition whirlpool of less than thoughtful spending, and before we know it, if you're like me, you ask, where has all the money gone? As I write, the fluctuating savings rate is actually negative—meaning that the average American is spending more than she is making (the rate is even higher for twenty-somethings).

We've lost touch with the word 'enough' and are utterly out of touch with how most people live their lives. Call it a 'crisis of humanity'—we're almost oblivious to the fact that the majority of the world lives in inhuman conditions. Madison Avenue is not going to tell us this. Hollywood is not going to tell us this. But Jesus is.

The Bible tells us the human face of Jesus is found in the poor. Jesus called them 'the least of these.' (Matt. 25).

One of the gifts my church has offered me is an opportunity to talk frankly and openly about my relationship to money.

After all, it's not really my money.

The word 'steward' comes from the old English word 'sty-ward.' It refers to the person who watches over the pigsty, which is not only poetically ironic, but was and still is in some places, a pretty important job.

In a very real sense this word connotes a tending to and caring for our most valuable possessions.

In the same way, Episcopalians consider stewardship to be the proper and generous use of our time, talent and treasure. On a grand scale we see our stewardship as all that we do with our lives after saying 'I believe.' We understand that God doesn't want our money nearly as much as God wants us to be joyful and generous givers of all that we have. God wants to shape us into generous people.

North Americans especially need to realize our call to philanthropy and generosity on a global scale. Episcopalians strive to understand the discipline of supporting the parish to be just such an exercise. We realize that the more we give to our parishes, the more our parishes can give to those who need it.

Most churches raise money each year in a parish-wide drive called a stewardship campaign (though some parishioners fondly refer to it

Small change = Big change

In 1889 a group of Episcopal women started the United Thank Offering. It encourages Episcopalians to give thanks by giving to charity. The UTO passes out little blue boxes and asks us to add money every time we feel blessed. Once the money is tallied, grants totaling two to three million dollars are given out each year.

Get your little blue box at:
www.episcopalchurch.org/uto

as a beg-a-thon). It's usually in the fall. We talk about money. We preach about money. We remind ourselves that money is not a secular issue, it's a spiritual issue. Only money touches on our deepest convictions of identity, purpose, idolatry and self-worth. It's not always a comfortable conversation. Most parishes ask members to sign a pledge card. Once these cards are turned in, we draw up a budget and pray we can keep our promises. Part of the budget goes to our regional and national leadership (more on page 145) to help fund programming, relief efforts and other activities.

The standard for giving in the Episcopal Church is ten percent of gross earnings. It's called a 'tithe.' This is a long-standing tradition in the Church, recently formalized in a resolution by our General Convention (a church-wide legislative body that meets every three years). It encourages all Episcopalians, "to develop a personal spiritual discipline that includes, at the minimum, the holy habits of tithing, daily personal prayer and study, Sabbath time and weekly corporate worship."[5]

Death and Taxes

They're life's unavoidables. Find out where your taxes go:
http://nationalpriorities.org/auxiliary/interactivetaxchart/taxchart.html

---

In reality, the giving level in my church, like most others, is much less. We're not where we would like to be, and this is one of our many flaws. But like countless other churches, we're trying. And our desire to be the best Christ-followers we can be is why our church communities are so vital. We have to expand our conversation about money and the things that shape our lives beyond ourselves. We realize we're called to join countless others in this difficult talk—we can't do it alone.

It's about community. It's about humility.

It's about being the Body of Christ. And it's about using all three to help shape us into the kind of people we want to be.

8. WORD

The Bible must not always be taken literally,
though it must always be taken seriously.

Word

Around the turn of the millennium I remember clipping a newspaper article. The paper had called together a group of experts to talk about building a time capsule.[1] The editors wanted to know the best way to pass on information that would last one thousand years—from the year 2000 to the year 3000.

"We're leaning toward some sort of digital capsule. What do you think?" they asked the panel.

"Digital is a problem," said a conservation consultant, "Digital storage media—floppies, compact discs, whatever—don't have a long life span—a few decades at most. Analog is the way you should go."

So the panelists debated photographs, vinyl records, data etched on expensive metals and other things before a paper conservation expert chimed in. "Don't forget about paper," she said. The panel warmed up to the idea as she noted paper's impressive track record, "Some papers have lasted for more than a thousand years, under the right conditions, acid-free paper can last for a long time," she continued.

Later, the question of the capsule's storage came up.

Where do we put this thing once we've packed it?

This prompted lots of questions:

Should we bury the capsule? Where?

How do we mark its location without encouraging looters?

What about earthquakes, rising water tables and changes in governments and national boundaries?

"What we really need is a 'priesthood'" suggested a physics professor, "people who will worship and take care of the capsule. A stable institution like a synagogue… would protect it and move it when they go. You can count on cultural institutions to be conservative and last the longest."

Wow, I thought.

That's how we got the Bible.

Inspired words scratched in stone, on animal skins, papyrus, and paper, hidden in caves, buried in cellars, copied by scribes, defended by monks, cherished and preserved through two millennia by cultural institutions that somehow survived wars, famines, invasions, droughts and persecutions.

This is how the Bible found its way to our bookshelves. It's a miraculous and mysterious book, a wonder-filled and wonder-working collection of stories, poems, songs, history and wisdom that Christians have always believed holds the keys to salvation.

Why would so many people go through so much trouble to safeguard this book? What makes this book worth dying for?

To a sizeable percentage of everyone who's ever walked the face of the earth the answer is simple.

The Bible is God speaking to us.

Bible Church

Like other Christians, Episcopalians firmly root their faith on the Gospel of Jesus Christ as revealed in the Bible.

It's the foundation of all we do. In fact, you could argue that Episcopalians and our spiritual parent, the Church of England, have done more to promote the Bible than any other body of Christians.

Forgive me if it sounds obvious, but the Church of England brought us the English Bible.

Some five centuries ago, the Church of England's theologians and leaders saw to it that every parish would replace their Latin Bibles with English versions—and that everybody in the parish, not just clergy was allowed to read the Bible.

As the English empire grew, the English Bible, especially the King James Version, went around the world.

How to Read the Bible

1) Begin with the Gospel of Mark
2) Read it alongside a reference book (called a "Commentary")
3) Read it in several different translations
4) Read it with a class
5) Take it seriously, not literally
6) Worship God, not the Bible.

Today, North Americans are obsessed with the English Bible.

Since the King James Version, there have been no less than 500 English translations. Americans buy about 25 million copies of the Bible each year (twice as many as your average Harry Potter book debut), to the tune of some $500 million.

Ninety-one percent of our homes have at least one Bible—the average home has four.

And the U.S.-based Gideon's International gives away a new Bible every second of every day.[2]

The English Bible has influenced more people (and more politics) than any other book that's ever been written.

Our prayer book spells out our devotion to Scripture. Shortly after the Episcopal Church was established, we followed the Church of England's lead and adopted the Articles of Religion (they're in the back of the prayer book). Article VI says that Holy Scripture "containeth all things necessary to salvation... whatsoever is not read therein, nor may be proved thereby, is not required of any man." (The Book of Common Prayer, page 868)

At all Episcopal ordinations, deacons, priests, and bishops are obliged to attest to this 'Oath of Conformity' as a part of their vows: "I solemnly declare that I do believe the

Where Do Sunday's Bible Readings Come From?

Episcopalians, like other liturgical churches, hear a lot of Bible readings on Sundays. We follow a three-year cycle of readings called the Revised Common Lectionary. We share this Lectionary with Roman Catholics, Presbyterians, Lutherans and many of the world's Christians. Following a lectionary allows us to hear all of the Bible, the full gospel. It keeps us from picking and choosing certain favorite texts while avoiding the harder ones.

Holy Scriptures of the Old and New Testaments to be the word of God and to contain all things necessary to salvation."

Though I've never seen it advertised this way, the Episcopal Church is a Bible church.

We believe that in matters of faith, nothing plays a more central role than the Holy Scriptures. Most of us consider ourselves well within the realm of biblical orthodoxy as it has been handed down to us, and we continue to cherish the Bible as our foundation.

Episcopalians show this devotion in the way we worship.

On any given Sunday four readings are heard at most of our church services: an Old Testament reading, a Psalm, a New Testament reading and a Gospel reading. Our prayers are laden with scriptural ideas, metaphors and quotes. When Scripture isn't being directly quoted, our worship services are bathed in biblical imagery.

Sunday's assigned readings are arranged so that the major portions of the Bible are read in the congregation every three years.

Those who are faithful to the morning and evening prayers suggested in the prayer book, (more on page 102), find that over a two-year period they read an even bigger portion of Scripture. In fact, the Book of Psalms is read several times. While reading Scripture is vital to every Christian's growth, it is reading Scripture together that has always played a central role in our use of the Bible.

Interpretation

We all know the Bible is complicated.

We've all heard about wild interpretations that have led to some far-out consequences.

The Bible is really not a book at all, but a collection of books. These were written over hundreds of years by a number of very different authors.

It's understandable that there would be some discrepancies.

For example, in Genesis the Bible tells us two different stories of Creation and two rival accounts of how the Israelites got their first king. The writer of Deuteronomy argues that good is always rewarded and that evil is always punished, which is countered by the contrary experiences of Job; the argument against taking foreign wives in Ezra and Nehemiah is countered by the righteous life of the foreigner Ruth who was blessed in her marriage to an Israelite. Most scholars agree that Scripture itself has corrected earlier versions of Scripture in some cases, "and in other cases, rival arguments were allowed to stand side by side unresolved."[3] It's no wonder that Scripture has been used to justify everything from slavery to apartheid to the oppression of women. Let's face it, when someone says, 'The Bible plainly says...' we are more likely hearing, 'My interpretation of the Bible tells me...'

So how do we make sense of the Bible's apparent contradictions and its long-time use as a proof text to just about every political agenda?

How do we discern God's Word for us today out of this ancient and hard-to-figure-out collection of books?

Can we really take the Bible seriously?

Of course we can. We all know that interpreting the Bible is hard work. Disagreement on a wide variety of issues exists.
Even Episcopalians don't agree on any one way to interpret the Bible.
However, most of us operate from two strong convictions:

1) we read the Bible together, and
2) we do so reasonably and responsibly.

If I had to choose just one word to describe how Episcopalians read the Bible it would have to be community. We believe no one person has full knowledge of the Scriptures. We believe the truth arises when everybody gets his or her say. It's a conviction we've held for some time, "both for [the] first generation of Anglicans and for Anglicans today, the Bible was not meant to be studied in isolation."[4]

The idea that any one person reading the Bible without calling on the expert knowledge of the theologian or priest, (or the unique viewpoints of the retired widow or skateboarding teenager), is actually objectionable to most of us. I like the comment by an Anglican theologian who was arguing with the Puritans in the sixteenth century and declared, "Bare reading [provides] bare feeding [for hungry souls]."[5]

We also believe that just as you and I might take a class to learn more about interpreting Shakespeare—or read a book about how to build a sun deck on the back of the house—Episcopalians commonly study with experts, taking classes and reading commentaries as ways of approaching the Bible. We believe that, "like all books, the Bible has a history that determines how it should be read.

It is a history that must be learned and its boundaries respected.

We cannot read into the Bible what was never there. Nor can we simply pick and choose the texts that meet our needs or reinforce our prejudices, wresting passages out of context and turning them into slogans."[6]

The Bible was written by particular people in particular places with particular agendas. We believe it's reasonable to take the Bible's context seriously, and by context, we mean:

- The context of public worship where the Bible has been heard, prayed and preached;

- The context of ancient cultures and languages where the Bible first was written and published;

- The context of tradition, especially that of the first four centuries of Christianity, where characteristically Christian methods of reading the Bible began to take shape;

- The context of almost two thousand years of intellectual, scientific, religious and social change. For it is here that, in diverse times and places, Episcopalians along with other Christians have wrestled with the meaning of the Bible in our lives.[7]

Reading the Bible responsibly is one big reason Episcopalians cherish common sense.

It not only makes for solid interpretation, but it gives it the dignity, majesty and worth this great book so dearly deserves.

Refusing to grapple with the Bible's intricacies, ambiguities and tensions can get us into trouble.

It can hurt us.

Or worse.

Club

I was having lunch with my friend Heather the other day. She was telling me about her best friend. When they were kids they went to the same school but different churches.

Whenever Heather slept over at her friend's house she was expected to go to church with the family on Sunday morning. But whenever her friend slept over at Heather's she wouldn't go to Heather's church.

Her parents said it was because Heather's church wasn't a 'real' church. They didn't read the Bible the same way. Her parents said people who went to Heather's church weren't going to heaven.

Most of us know stories like Heather's.

Episcopal churches are full of them. Remember, two out of three of our members are converts. Many of us have sad stories about our experiences with other Christians.

Many of us have sad stories about our experiences with interpretations of the Bible that were condemning, hurtful and abusive.

Many of us have come to the Episcopal Church because we try pretty hard not to use the Bible as a club.

When it comes to reading the Bible, Episcopalians are very wary of rigid, literal interpretations.

"Brother, Are You Saved?"

It's a question some Christians like to ask and we have our own answer.

At the heart of the Episcopal Church is a positive response to Christ's call to 'follow me.' Romans 10:9 says, "if you confess with your lips that Jesus is Lord and believe in your heart that God raised him from the dead, you will be saved." Episcopalians believe we have not only done this at our baptism (if not before) but that we are continually accepting Christ into our hearts every time we take Communion.

We understand salvation as a process and a journey, not a one-time event. Our differences with other Christians are usually over language, not belief - a former Archbishop of Canterbury once answered the question this way,

"I have been saved, I am being saved, I hope to be saved."

Do we take the Bible literally?

Sure ("love thy neighbor").

Do we take all of the Bible literally?

No (When John the Baptist called Jesus the "Lamb of God," he was probably not suggesting that Mary had a little Lamb). We realize that people tend to interpret the Bible to say what they want it to say—kind of like a drunk uses a lamppost: more for support than illumination.

We may not mean to. But we all do it.

And when that happens, the Bible, the most profound testament to God's extraordinary love, loses its power for good.

It can hurt, it can maim and it can destroy.

It can become a club—and nobody likes that.

This is why we tend to be open-minded about the Bible. We read it together so that one person's interpretation doesn't take us off the deep end. We look to modern scholarship to tell us about new discoveries in science, literature and archeology.

We expect Scripture to be handled with the same kind of scholarship we afford any other great literary work. We're not nearly as inclined to 'circle the wagons' as we are to open up the party, welcoming new ways of looking at Scripture as a community.

And we delight in the way our Episcopal heritage and contributions are being used to further the healing work so many people are doing.

We join Christians of every age who have cherished the Bible.

It's a revolutionary manifesto showing us a radical new way of life.

It's a magical invitation to meet the love of our lives.

It's a family album meant for all God's people to treasure and adore.

It's a solemn repository of our true identity—telling us who we really are.

And, perhaps most importantly, its God speaking to us today—which is why the Bible will never need a time capsule.

9. MAP

'How lovely!
It has so many nice quotes from the Prayer Book.'

Episcopalian after reading the Bible

Map

I have a dear friend named Judith.
She loves to meet people.
She loves to help people.

Many Sundays she stands at the back of the church scouting for anyone who's joining the community for worship for the first time. When she finds somebody she introduces herself and offers to guide her new friend through the service.

She knows that new people can have a hard time following along. So she grabs a prayer book, sits with them throughout the service and helps people find their way.

Judith is our Map Lady.

As devoted to the Bible as Episcopalians are, if you walk into a typical church on a typical Sunday and look inside a pew you probably won't find one. But you will find another book:

The Book of Common Prayer.

More than any other group of Christians, Episcopalians are a people of the book. This book has a profound affect on how we pray and what we believe. It shapes our souls, sculpts our worship, and encourages us to engage in the ongoing and sacred conversation with the Almighty that we all know as prayer.

If the Christian life is a journey, The Book of Common Prayer is our map.

One way to describe the prayer book is to think of it as the Bible rearranged for worship. Its prayers and liturgies are rich with words and phrases from some of the most beloved Bible passages. Its order and simplicity open our hearts to the grandeur and wonder of God in our own special way. "Its texts and traditions point to a living tradition, a distinct way of being a Christian."[1]

It's also our gift to the world.

Book of Common Prayer junkies (like me) often recognize its finely crafted phrases in public and private ceremonies. I've heard it used in Presidential funerals, 'non-denominational' outdoor weddings—even soap operas.

I'm sure a lot of others borrow it too.

And we don't mind.

We're happy to do almost anything we can to help people pray. We believe the Lord inspired our prayer book so we could give it to you.

You can find copies of The Book of Common Prayer at most major bookstores. It is eloquent in voice, admirable in simplicity, and meticulous in detail. It is orthodox in theology and generous in spirit. Its precise terminology and economy of vocabulary has helped countless numbers of people talk with God and each other. The prayer book helps us pray in ways that spark our imaginations, enhance our communities, and at its core, feed our souls.

Lexes

A common phrase we use to describe the effect prayer has on us is embodied in a Latin saying, "Lex orandi, lex credendi."

It means that, "praying shapes believing."

In other words, the way we pray gives form to what we believe.

This differs from, say, Presbyterians, who have the Westminster Confession. Or Lutherans, who have the Augsburg Confession. Episcopalians have never had their own specific creed or confession. What we've always had is prayer, best expressed in our Book of Common Prayer. "The prayer book does not offer precise doctrinal formulations that must be adhered to, rather it provides the forms that outline our practice of the Christian faith, shaped principally by worship."[2]

The important role The Book of Common Prayer plays is probably best measured by the degree of pandemonium caused when it is changed. Our current prayer book was adopted, after years of study and debate, in 1979 and before that, updated in 1928. The process of changing the prayer book is never pretty (most priests I know quietly pray they'll retire before a new one comes out).

This dissention is largely caused because Episcopalians understand that changing our prayers changes what we believe.

Here's an example: A major revision in our most recent prayer book (the 1979 version) changed the way people prayed before receiving communion. The change asked worshippers to pray that they've been made righteous through Christ and are, "worthy to stand before you." (BCP 368)

This contrasted with the old prayer (the 1928 version), which had emphasized our unworthiness. It read, "We are not worthy so much as to gather the crumbs from under thy table." (BCP 337) While this change seemed new, it was actually a return to a much older prayer—from the third century when Christians were much more apt to celebrate Christ's victory over death and the gift of right standing with God. Some people took quite a while to accept the change. A few still haven't. The new prayer book has a different spirituality. Although for many of us, it has become a deeper spirituality.[3]

While many of us may not like change, we know that the world changes. Our language changes, our problems change and our insights change. This affects how we interpret the Bible. Today, Hebrew and Greek scholars translate the Bible with greater accuracy and modern archaeologists cast new light on Biblical times. That's why Bible translations are updated, and that's why the prayer book always follows suit. As theologian Leonel Mitchell puts it, "The language of theology must be able to hear and respond to these new experiences without changing

What About the Creeds?

Episcopalians also cherish the historic Creeds. We recite the Apostles' Creed at Baptisms, Morning Prayer, and Evening Prayer. We use the Nicene Creed at the Eucharist, usually on Sunday mornings. According to the Articles of Religion, passed in 1801, "The Nicene Creed, and that which is commonly called the Apostles' Creed, ought thoroughly to be received and believed: for they may be proved by most certain warrants of Holy Scripture." (BCP 869)

its age-old witness to the eternal, unchanging God."[4]

Origins

If the idea of a prayer book sounds old fashioned, it is.
It is very old fashioned. It has very deep roots.

As I've mentioned, the very first Christians were Jews and based their worship on an inherited Hebrew tradition. They gathered during the day to hear Scripture read and then explained. This was followed by a distinctively Christian element—an Agape, or love feast. It was an evening event commemorating the last supper—sharing the bread and wine according to Jesus' instructions. Over time, the two traditions came together and formed one. As Christianity spread, these rituals evolved and different prayers and liturgies were created for days (other than Sundays) and events (like weddings and funerals).

They were collected and written in books called missals. These were the earliest prayer books. They eventually grew to include liturgies for prayer five or even seven times a day.

With the arrival of the Middle Ages missals had grown so lengthy and complex they became absolutely impossible to use unless you had all day to devote to prayer—like a monk, a nun, or a priest.

Then there was the problem of language.

While missals were used in different countries where a number of different languages were spoken, most of these books were written in Latin.

In England this practice dramatically changed following the Reformation. In 1549, during the reign of young Edward VI, the first Book of Common Prayer was published—in English.

Vast changes were made, especially in the daily prayers. The new prayer book called for daily prayer just two times a day, morning and evening. The idea was to make the book accessible to common people. That's how the word 'common' became part of the title.

As battles raged between Protestants and Catholics in England, new prayer books reflected the biases of whoever was on the throne. These books were introduced in 1552, 1559, 1604 and finally 1662, the last of which is still the official prayer book of the Church of England. However, many alternative liturgies have been approved since then—and that's what we find in use in most English churches today.

It was this 1662 Book of Common Prayer that was first used in American colonies.

But following the Revolutionary War and the founding of the Episcopal Church, we needed a new prayer book. We needed one that didn't, among other things, require Americans to pray for the King of England. Our first prayer book was a slight revision of the 1662 version and it was approved in 1789. New American prayer books followed in 1892, 1928, then 1979, which is the book found in most Episcopal parishes today.

The First Prayer Book

In 1549, under Edward VI, (Henry VIII's son), the primary language of public worship changed from Latin to English.

The first Book of Common Prayer was used Pentecost Sunday, June 9, 1549, and the occasion is still commemorated, "on the first convenient day following Pentecost."

Test Drive

Many of the questions you might have about how Episcopalians pray and what we believe are in the The Book of Common Prayer. It's 1,001 pages long and is scientifically engineered to be just thick enough to fit into that rack on the back of most church pews.

It is poetry. It is prose. It is brilliant. And it has a way of inviting us into a deeper understanding of God's plan for us through Jesus.

- *So here's what you'll find when you open the prayer book:*
- *Daily Prayers* – Morning and evening prayers, also called offices, can be used by yourself, with a friend, or in a congregation. One version, Rite I, uses a traditional voice and the other version, Rite II, is more contemporary.

- **Collects** – These prayers are 'collections' of thoughts, hence the word 'collect' (pronounced KAH-leckt). Again, there are two versions of each, traditional and contemporary. There is one for each Sunday of the year and each Holy Day as well as collects for special occasions, like birthdays and special needs such as unemployment and sickness.

- **Liturgies for Special Days** – For Episcopalians, like most Christians,Easter is the highlight of the year. The liturgies, from Ash Wednes-day through Holy Week are placed toward the beginning of the prayer book to signify their importance to us.

- **Holy Baptism** – Episcopalians baptize babies as well as adults. We usually do so on certain Sundays as part of the regular worship ser-vices. Parishes differ in their customs. Some sprinkle water, others dunk candidates under water. In this section you can find out how we do baptisms and what we believe about them.

- **Holy Eucharist** – In this section you'll find out what goes on in the main Sunday services at most Episcopal churches. Rite I services are more traditional. They're usually the earliest services offered at parishes on any given Sunday. They usually don't include music. Rite II services are more contemporary. Many parishes consider this their main service. They often include music. If you've never attended an Episcopal Church, this part of the prayer book is something you might want to read before you go.

- **Pastoral Offices** – Episcopalians mark life's important events like confirmation, marriage, reconciliation, prayer for the sick, and funerals with some exquisite liturgy. You can find these services here.

- **The Psalter** – One of the distinctions of Episcopal worship is that many of our parishes sing the Psalms. Psalm comes from the Greek psalmos, a translation of a Hebrew word, zmr, which means 'to pluck.' The Psalms were originally composed to be accompanied by a lyre or harp. The prayer book has a special version of the Psalms that makes them easier to put to music.

- **Catechism** – What do Episcopalians believe? This part of the prayer book uses a question and answer format to explain the Episcopal Church's beliefs.

- *Lectionaries* – These are Bible reading calendars. Certain passages are appointed for certain days. By following this schedule, much of the Bible can be read both individually, (see the Daily Office Lectionary) and corporately (see The Lectionary).

Daily

The alarm clock went off before sunrise. I got into my car, put the top down, and began making my way up the canyon. Higher and higher I climbed, winding around the mountain, cool breeze waking me up, until the sun was about to pop up over the horizon. I pulled over just in time to see the first rays of sunshine hit the mountaintop. It was incredible. I grabbed my Bible and prayer book. I hiked a short way to the overlook and sat down.

I gazed out over the city. That view—the juxtaposition of nature with the skyline, illuminated by a fantastically clear day—was one of the most amazing sites I had ever seen.

God's creation. God's city.
God's presence—so real.
And I had my part to play.

I came to pray.

Few of our prayer times are this dramatic. Maybe yours come on an easy chair in the living room, at the kitchen table over a cup of coffee, at bedtime, or during a break at work. Some of these are really memorable. Some of them aren't. But every one of them is really important.

I have found few resources that can make my daily devotions more fulfilling than the prayer book. It's my time to connect with God.

It's my time to realign my priorities and to center. It's my sacred time when I join millions of Christians the world over who share these moments of divine meditation.

Many Episcopalians begin the day using a morning prayer liturgy found in the prayer book. I usually use Rite II. Morning prayer is dedicated to Bible reading and prayer. Although we often use this liturgy at church, with a few alterations it can easily be used individually.

Here's one way: First, I find a quiet place where I can be alone, or at least undisturbed for a period of time. Many people light candles or incense and arrange their worship spaces in appropriate ways, which is great if you can do it. Other people go outside, surrounded by nature. The Morning Prayer liturgy works anywhere.

It'll take from ten minutes to an hour (or more) depending on the Scriptures chosen; any additional readings, and the time spent praying. The prayer book's job is to give us a framework for our worship. It's OK to include outside readings, meditations and songs. Certain things can also be left out. Focusing our hearts and minds on Christ is the main thing.

Once settled, the Daily Morning Office begins on page 75.

(At this point you may want to grab a Prayer Book and follow along.)

We start with an Opening sentence. The sentence reflects the particular season of the Christian year. This helps settle our souls and concentrate on the moment. Skip to page 79 for the confession then head to the Psalter on the next page.

After reading an appropriate sentence, we're invited to say, sing or chant one of the three ancient prayers on pages 82-83. These are really old hymns that have kept their Latin titles. Venite means 'come,' Jubilate means 'be joyful,' and Pascha Nostrum means 'Christ our Passover.'

Following these hymns, the Psalm or Psalms appointed may be read, chanted or sung.

The Psalms are followed by the day's readings.

Finding the day's readings can be tricky. They're contained in The Daily Office Lectionary found on page 934. It may be hard to understand at first, but it becomes easier over time. It helps to be somewhat familiar with the Church Year (see page 71). One way to find the appropriate week is to look at the Sunday church bulletin—many parishes print the appropriate week right on the cover.

An Anglican mystic once wrote, "Spiritual reading is, or at least can be, second only to prayer as a developer and support to the inner life."[5] At this point it is appropriate to read more than the daily Scriptures like a Bible commentary or another book.

Following the readings the songs of the saints, called canticles, are sung. Page 85 begins with Canticle 8. Canticles 1-7 are on pages 47-52. One or more of these can be said or sung as part of the Office. Or not.

Right here is where our liturgy takes a big turn. We go from Bible reading to prayer. It begins with the "Our Father" on page 97. Suggested prayers, called suffrages, follow—'A' or 'B' can be prayed.

Collects appropriate to the Office are next. The prayer book gives us freedom to choose one or more, or our own.

The liturgy allows for lots of flexibility in prayer because personal prayer is just that—personal.

While the prayers of the ancients are certainly helpful, they may not always be. Feel free to create or find your own prayers.

Morning prayer can end in different ways, with a hymn, or an anthem, or with one the concluding sentences on page 102.

Praying according to a formal liturgy may seem awkward for the uninitiated. It was for me.

However, a quiet time for prayer, meditation and study is often the most fulfilling part of my day. Most Episcopalians are humbled and delighted to know that the prayer book plays such an important role in the shaping of Christian souls.

It's a guide to us on our journeys. It's a light unto our paths.

We thank God for giving us such a good map.

10. ROOTS

Christianity would be in far better shape today if we would simply remember to read the minutes from the previous meetings.

John Krumm

Roots

Imagine you've just drawn a horizontal line on a chalkboard.
It represents the age of the universe (unknown, but billions of years old).

Then put a vertical mark on the line to show when humans first appeared (rough estimate: 1,200,000 years ago).

Through the years many admirable people have called the Anglican or the Episcopal Church their home, here are some of them:

Literary Figures and Artists

Jane Austen, Charles Dickens, John Donne, T.S. Eliot, Madeline L'Engle, C.S. Lewis, William Faulkner, Georgia O'Keefe, William Shakespeare, John Steinbeck, Harriet Beecher Stowe, Tennessee Williams

Politicians and Public Figures

Princess Diana, Queen Elizabeth, Winston Churchill, Madeline Albright, John Danforth, Eleanor Roosevelt, Fiorella La Guardia, Colin Powell, J.P. Morgan, the Mellons, the Vanderbilts

- One-quarter of U.S. Presidents have been Episcopalians, more than any other denomination. Including George Washington, Thomas Jefferson, Franklin D. Roosevelt, and George H. W. Bush.
- Three-quarters of the signers of the Declaration of Independencewere Anglican layman.
- Roughly one-third of all U.S. Supreme Court Justices have been Episcopalians, far more than any other denomination, including: Thurgood Marshall, Sandra Day O'Connor, and David Souter.
- Episcopalians commanded forty-two seats in the 109th Congress,about thirty-three more than their current share of the U.S. population would warrant.[3]

Science and Health

Charles Darwin, Margaret Mead, Florence Nightingale, Jeanette Piccard

Entertainers

Natalie Cole, Judy Collins, Judy Garland, Charlie Chaplin, Bono, Rosanne Cash, Moby, Laurence Olivier, Sam Waterston, Fred Astaire, Robin Williams, Susan Sarandon, Courtney Cox-Arquette

Put another mark where humans with brains the size of ours surfaced (about 500,000 years ago).

Put another mark where civilization popped up (10,000-12,000 years ago, after the continental ice sheets retreated).

Finally put a mark where Christ appeared (2,000 years ago).

Now step back and see how young humanity is. Now step back and see how really young Christianity is. Christianity is one of the youngest of all the major world religions. Only Islam is younger.

While some religions have flourished, others have faded. One historian points out that Buddhism and Confucianism have declined over the last 500 years while Islam is on the rise.

Christianity is currently at an apex of popularity. "In spite of many adversaries and severe losses… [Christianity] has become more deeply rooted among more peoples than it or any other faith has ever been before. It is also more widely influential in the affairs of men than any other religious system which mankind has known."[1]

Every day thousands of people around the world are baptized and hundreds of new churches are started. In the U.S., a new church is planted every two hours.[2] Christianity is sweeping through many parts of Africa, Asia and Latin America. One-third of the world professes Christianity.

Yet, in spite of this growth some people predict Christianity will eventually fade away. They point out declines in European churchgoing and the rise of atheism (today, 'no religion' is the fourth largest "religion.")

But regardless of where Christianity is or goes, the New Testament seems to be clear about the Lord's purposes for the world. The Bible tells us that God set a plan in motion for all of creation, which had a beginning and will have an end.

Christians often use the Greek word telos, which means goal or target. The Christian story tells us that all of creation is on a trajectory and holds distinctive purpose, meaning and telos.

In writing to Christians in Ephesus in the first century St. Paul explained that Jesus plays an integral part in that plan. Paul says that God waited until the fullness of time to send His Son, "in accordance with the eternal purpose" that God established (Ephesians 3:11). Paul argues that as sure as there is a world, there is a God and this God has a plan. Christianity may amble along in fits and starts for thousands of years. But eventually God will bring to fruition in Christ a climax to 'all things seen and unseen.'

Christians believe all of history has a divine rationale—there's a reason for everything. Bound up somewhere along this chalkboard timeline are our lives.

We have our own places in history. We have our own calling and mission. We have our own ways of being Christian in this new millennium.

And the way we live into the future is helped to no end by what we've learned from the past. Episcopalians value and adore our heritage. We're inheritors of an amazing story that's been handed down to us in a very distinctive way—and we realize that to fully appreciate what's new, we need to understand what's old.

Or in this case, what's ancient.

Beginnings

One of the common questions Episcopalians get is, 'Who founded your church'?' Most people think it was Henry VIII.

Some people think it was Elizabeth I.

But we all know it was Jesus Christ.

The Episcopal Church has no creeds or beliefs of its own. We inherited it all from Christianity's earliest days. We're simply one (of many) traditions within the Christian religion.

However, our road has certainly been one of intrigue and drama.

Many characters have played their roles in many historical settings. But the development of our church has been continual, without fundamental change of faith and order, since the time of the apostles who were ordained by Jesus himself. The New Testament tells us that following the life, death, and resurrection of Jesus, Christianity spread throughout the Middle East and into the countries around the Mediterranean Sea.

Merchants and Roman soldiers are probably the first to have brought the

Gospel to the shores of Britain, but exactly when and how is anybody's guess. Unauthenticated sources tell us the tall tale of Joseph of Arimet-hea, a man mentioned in the New Testament who donated his tomb for Christ's burial. Pious legend takes it from there—Joseph had also allegedly gained possession of 'the Holy Grail,' or the chalice used at the Last Supper, and come to Glaston-bury, England. While historians can verify little, if any, of this, it's certainly helped sell plenty of King Arthur's 'Knights of the Round Table' books, Monty Python DVDs, as well as membership subscriptions to the Chamber of Commerce of Glastonbury. A writer from North Africa named Tertullian wrote extensively about Early Christianity and is the first to mention the existence of Christians in England. In 200 AD he tells of parts of Britain that were inaccessible

What's in a Name?

Here are some common names we've all heard before but may not have known their Celtic Christian origins:

St. Aidan - A seventh century Irish monk who was sent out from Iona, Scotland, he successfully evangelized Northumbria and set up his mission at Lindesfarne.

St. Alban - He was a converted Roman soldier, and in the fourth century became England's first martyr by choosing death rather than give up a friend to persecutors.

St. Brigid - A fifth century Irish nun, known for her beauty, she was converted by St. Patrick and traveled much of the country evangelizing.

St. Chad - A seventh century English monk who became bishop of York earning a reputation of humility and prayerfulness.

St. Columba - A sixth century Irish monk, who was the son of royalty, served as an itinerant preacher throughout Ireland and Scotland.

St. David - The sixth century son of a Welsh king, he became head of the Church of Wales, founded monasteries and converted pagans.

St. Hilda - A seventh century English abbess (head of a monastery) who hosted the famous Synod of Whitby that made an important decision regarding the direction of the church in England' (see p. 114).

St. Patrick - Patrick was not actually Irish, but British (which no Irishman likes to hear on St. Patrick's Day). He traveled to Ireland in the fourth century where he evangelized the country, chased out the snakes, and became its patron saint.

Where Did All These Churches Come From?

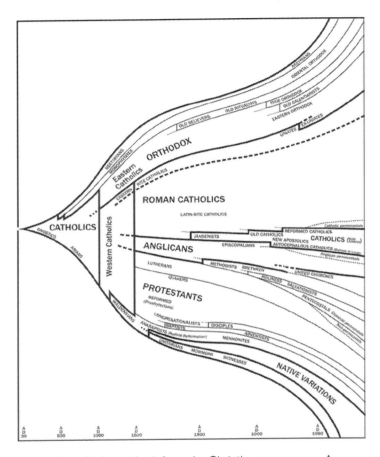

The point in the middle on the left marks Christ's appearance. As you move to the right you can see, marked by the years on the bottom, just how the Church has evolved. One thing that becomes very clear is that every church that has ever existed has participated in some sort of schism. No church is undivided. No one has a claim to purity and authenticity. Yes, we are all guilty of breaking unity with one another. And we all share in the conviction that Christ's 'One True Church' is not of human construction, but of God's.[4]

to the Romans that nevertheless had been "conquered by Christ."[5] One hundred years later we hear the story of St. Alban, England's first martyr. Alban was a third century Roman citizen and pagan, living in Britain, who took in a Christian priest on the run from soldiers persecuting him for his faith. They developed a friendship, and through the priest's instruction, Alban became a Christian. Soon after, soldiers came to Alban's house to arrest the priest. But Alban put on the priestly robes and surrendered himself to the soldiers in place of his friend. He was put to death in an act of Christian love.

It was during this third century that Christianity became somewhat organized in England. Historians tell us about three English bishops, all representing different dioceses who attended the Council of Arles in France in 304 AD.

Nearly a century later, in 401 AD, the Roman legions withdrew from England and Anglo-Saxon barbarians from Germany began their sporadic invasions. Over the next one hundred years their wars with Britons and Celts chased many Christians away. Some went west to Wales and Ireland. Some went north to Scotland. Finally, in the sixth century, when wars with British tribal kingdoms slowed, the re-conversion of England began.

It took on two distinct forms.

St. Columba launched a form of Celtic Christianity from Ireland that moved with him across the Irish Sea to Iona, Scotland.

A second mission, a Roman Catholic one, in 597 CE was established in the south at Canterbury and led by Augustine (not to be confused with the more famous Augustine of Hippo who lived a few hundred years earlier) after Pope Gregory sent a small group of monks from Rome.

Much of the country responded to these missions because by the time Columba and Augustine arrived, Christianity in Britain was at least 400 years old. England became more widely and more formally Christianized than ever, though somewhat divided into Celtic in the north and Roman in the South. Among their differences were separate dates for celebrating Easter and clergy haircuts (I'm not making this up). Tensions came to a head the in mid-seventh century when the King of Northumbria realized that he and his wife would be celebrating Easter at different times. He practiced the Celtic way. She practiced the Roman way. He'd had enough.

It was time to get everybody on the same page.

The king called a historic meeting called 'The Synod of Whitby.' The meeting would decide which brand of Christianity England would follow, Celtic or Roman. After hearing arguments on both sides, King Oswiu of Northumbria ruled in favor of Rome.

This was the direction that the rest of the world was going, he reasoned, and Britain would follow. "The Church of England [had now] brought herself in touch with the blood-stream of the Catholic Church and could henceforth play her full part in the life of Christendom."[6]

However, this decision didn't put an end to Celtic Christianity. It's still around today. Its liturgies, traditions, monasteries, abbeys and saints inspire our worship and formation in wonderful ways that we're continually re-discovering.

Reform

Over time England's bishops gradually found a home and acceptance in the Church of Rome. However, this reconciliation would not last through the Middle Ages.

The Roman Catholic Church was starting to enter a sad and unfortunate period of corruption. Endless stories of unscrupulous clergy, monks and popes infuriated Christians all over Europe. And with this outcry the fifteenth century began to feel the birth pangs of religious revolt and reformation. And England was not far behind. Taking center stage in this drama was one of history's most colorful figures, King Henry VIII.

Young Henry never planned to rule England. He was the second son of a father who had hoped Henry would become a churchman.

Then, Henry's older brother died.

And his father's plans for Henry changed, big time. Henry was to take his brother's throne. Henry was to take his brother's Spanish wife, Katherine of Aragon.

All this happened by the time he was seventeen.

Gifted in personality, good looks, athletics, intelligence, riches and political cunning, Henry was the consummate ruler.

His ambition was only outsized by his ego.

He was obsessed with cleanliness, fine dress, punctuality and order. He was the first English monarch who demanded to be called 'Your Majesty.'

Like the rulers of his time, Henry married for political gain and procreation, and had mistresses for pleasure.

Henry VIII was a doer.

He was a passionate builder of fine buildings, involved in the construction of King's Chapel in Cambridge and Westminster Abbey in London. He was also one of Eng-land's greatest patrons of the arts. However his craving for power, and preserving it, came to a

Henry and His Wives

The Church of England has had its colorful moments. Henry VIII shown here with his six brides. English school children remember their fates with this playful rhyme:

Divorced, beheaded, died.

Divorced, beheaded, survived

head in 1527. Henry had been married to Katherine for eighteen years and because of miscarriages and crib deaths had no male heir.

He started to believe that he had been cursed for marrying his brother's wife (which had required a papal dispensation). Henry had also fallen in love with the crafty Anne Boleyn, a member of the Queen's entourage.

And while Henry's marriage to Katherine had produced a daughter, he knew that a woman had never successfully ruled England.

Henry appealed to the Pope for an annulment.

Normally a fait accompli for people of Henry's stature, the annulment process was stalled by the Pope who didn't want to offend Katherine's uncle, the King of Spain, a powerful ruler at the time, who had the potential to do him great harm. After four years of waiting, Henry had enough.

He had already come up with plans to re-define his relationship with Rome. Soon Parliament declared Henry the Supreme Head of Church and State.

And not everyone was sad. Many people remembered that Rome had not always run their church. In fact, ever since William the Conqueror's arrival in the eleventh century, England's church had been in sporadic controversy with the Pope. As a result, some people saw Henry's move as a return to the English church's true heritage—it was a reversal of the Synod of Whitby.

Henry's actions meant that the huge wealth of English real estate owned by the Roman Catholic Church was now his. Sunday collections came under his power. Tragically, Henry ordered the destruction of ancient monasteries and gave church property to his friends.

Henry could now get married and divorced without the Pope's permission, which he did, going through a total of six wives. Henry continued to build England into a world power. He "began his reign in a medieval kingdom and ended his reign in a modern state."[7]

While it's widely believed that Henry the VIII founded the Church of England, Episcopalians don't like hearing this. Sure, it's bad history. But it also gives the false impression that Henry created the Church of England simply to accommodate his self-serving lifestyle and grandiose desire for power. The fact is that Henry never changed the fundamental doctrine and practice of the Church of Rome. The average English churchgoer didn't notice any difference under Henry's reign. Mass was still in Latin and there were still seven sacraments. Henry believed in the celibacy of priests, the Transubstantiation of the Eucharist, and the reverence of statues and icons. He lived and died a devout Catholic.

The real reformation of the Church of England would come from the powerful Protestant influences on the continent and from later monarchs, especially Henry's second daughter, Elizabeth I.

Frontier

Elizabeth. What a woman.

As I have mentioned, she's the person most responsible for the shape of the Church of England and by inheritance, the Episcopal Church.

During her reign:

- a compromised 'middle way' formed between Catholics and Protestants (see page 58)
- the Anglican Church's most revered theologian, Richard Hooker, defined the boundaries between Anglicans and Puritans—this is still important for us today, especially in our conversations with fundamentalists.
- the popular 1559 Book of Common Prayer was released.
- the Pope, in 1570, officially excommunicated the Church of England.

We're not too happy with this last one.

Yes, Henry provoked the Pope by declaring himself head of the English church, but he never wanted to break fellowship.

Today the break means that while baptized Roman Catholics are welcome to receive communion in Episcopal churches, Episcopalians are not officially extended the same invitation in Roman Catholic churches.

It's a rift with faults on both sides. Many Catholics and Anglicans pray every day for its healing, and our eventual re-uniting.

It was also in Elizabeth's reign that English explorers began making their way to the New World.

In 1579 on the shores of the Golden Gate Bay in San Francisco, a chaplain aboard the flagship of explorer Sir Francis Drake celebrated the first Book of Common Prayer service on American soil. The land grab was on among major European powers. Explorers from many different countries and faith traditions began staking their claims. The Puritans had New England. The Catholics had Florida and Maryland. The Baptists had Rhode Island. The Quakers had Pennsylvania and New Jersey. Swedish Lutherans had Delaware. The Dutch Reformed had New York. And the Church of England laid claim to Virginia, the Carolinas and Georgia.

Shortly after Elizabeth's reign ended England established its first permanent settlement here in America. It was in Virginia, which was named after Elizabeth, who was also known as the 'Virgin' Queen. There, in Jamestown in 1607, the Rev. Robert Hunt founded the first Church of England parish. Bruton Parish in Williamsburg, Virginia is the direct descendant of this church and you can still visit it today. From there the Church of England spread into Maryland and pretty much every major city along the coast. The church had its enemies because it also represented the English monarchical presence. This was the main hurdle to its growth because so many people had come to America to escape religious persecution.

But the church's progress was also hindered because we didn't have any bishops. The Bishop of London, who had never set foot in the New World, governed the church from afar. Even worse, the church wouldn't allow Americans to consecrate their own bishop. This meant nobody was being confirmed and anybody who wanted to be ordained had to make the long and dangerous trip back to England. In the eighteenth century, transatlantic voyages took the lives of one in five candidates for ordination.

As I look back at these devout clergy who braved those harsh conditions to shore up a badly limping church, I'm overcome with emotion. They took the same vows. They prayed the same prayers. Many of them gave their lives so that we might carry on the Lord's unfinished business. Four hundred years ago things were rough for my church.

But these men and women didn't give up. God didn't give up. There was a new church to start in a new land. Our ancient faith had already survived incredible twists, turns, changes, and reforms.

And it was being made new all over again.

11. ROPES

"The important thing is this:
To be able at any moment to sacrifice what we are
for what we could become."

Charles Dubois

Ropes

One night I was working as a chaplain at a youth retreat when a youngster named Diana asked if we could talk. She was stressed. She started to tell me about a good friend of hers. She'd known him for years but now she wanted to end the friendship. He had started doing something she highly disapproved of. She was convinced that her friend was destroying his life—and he was going to ruin the lives of many others.

She wanted to know if there was any way they could continue their friendship. I remember saying that it all depended on what he was doing... as my mind began to race—heroin, abortion, Columbine... She looked around to make sure no one was listening. Then she slowly turned to me, leaned in and whispered, "He has a can of chewing tobacco!"

I tried to keep a straight face.

I took a deep breath and we started to talk about the phases we go through as we grow up. We like certain toys, we like certain music and we do certain things that are really important to us at the time. But as we get older most of these things change. Diana and I talked about perspective. Diana and I talked about the perspective older people can give us, like our parents and grandparents who would likely tell us that her friend's decision to chew tobacco was a passing stage.

Parents and predecessors help guide us along. They've got a broader perspective. They've been there before. They know the ropes.

This is why history is so important to us. The lives and stories of those who have gone before us continue to teach and inspire us.

Episcopalians are inheritors of a specific tradition shaped by generations of people who've spent their lives facing many of the same things we now face. The story of our church's settlement and growth in North America is just such a story. This history, written and spoken, shows us the ropes—helping us to blaze pioneering paths into this new millennium.

Rebirth

During the American Revolution, the Episcopal Church was on the same shaky ground as the rest of the country. Most of our southern clergy stayed loyal to England. Most northern clergy sided with the new Americans. Northern loyalists either headed back to England or immigrated to Canada.

Clergy who remained faced stiff opposition from people who were suspicious of their historical alliance with the Church of England.

Clergy pay, which was sent from England, now stopped. In every state, except Connecticut, a shortage of clergy and parishioners meant most parishes were either closed or drastically understaffed. The future of the Episcopal Church looked dim at best although the majority of the signers of the Declaration of Independence were members.

Stability in Connecticut played a crucial role in the rebirth of the church. Seven years after the American Revolution, Connecticut parishes elected Samuel Seabury as their bishop. Hoping the uneasy feelings over the war had ended,

Samuel Seabury

He was the first bishop of the Episcopal Church. He served as a chaplain during the Revo-lutionary War and was con-secrated Bishop of Connecticut in 1784. He also served as Bishop of Rhode Island and as Presiding Bishop. Seabury-Western Seminary in Chicago was named after him.

Seabury sailed to England to be consecrated. It takes the laying on of hands of three bishops to make a new bishop, and America had none. But once in England, Seabury discovered he couldn't accept consecration. He would've had to take an oath of allegiance to the King. Frustrated, Seabury went north, to Scotland where he had once studied medicine. In Aberdeen, Scotland on November 14, 1784, three Scottish Episcopal bishops laid hands on Seabury and consecrated him as the first bishop of the Episcopal Church.

A few years later, after political changes in England, two other Americans, William White and Samuel Provoost, were consecrated bishops in London. Now the Episcopal Church had three bishops, enough to move forward on its own. In 1789 our first General Convention and the adoption of a new constitution, prayer book and name took place. The church was now called the Protestant Episcopal Church in America. These changes didn't begin a new tradition as much as carry on what had been handed down to us in the novel context of an independent nation. We didn't change any essential part of our heritage, not doctrine, discipline, or worship.

Now the Church was ready to grow.

Pioneer

Our growth didn't come easily or immediately.

Like the Church of England, many of our parishes faced a stagnating threat called Deism. This widely popular understanding depicted God as a distant observer who set the world in motion but had very little interest in intervening in the affairs of humankind. Divine moral law and moral behavior were at its center as well as a belief in God based on nature and reason rather than revelation through Holy Scripture.

With Deism strong, the Episcopal Church lacked the missionary zeal of Methodist and Baptist ministers. Droves of them were jetting out into the far-flung, Wild West frontier. With little more than a horse, a backpack, and a Bible, they set up tent meetings and churches in nearly every corner of the land. This evangelism was largely absent in our church for a full generation following the revolution.

My friends joke about it—saying that the Episcopalians waited for the trains.

Of course this wasn't entirely true. In time, devoted, pioneer missionaries, like Bishops Kemper and Griswold from New England, Bishops Moore and Meade from Virginia, and notably Bishop Hobart from New York, jumped into action. They were tenacious in handling the incredible growth and need around them.

Bishop John Hobart was the leading pioneer bishop.

He was a short man with glasses and a really nagging ulcer. Nonetheless, he was indefatigable. He was a smart and gentle preacher with the heart of a pastor.

Following his ordination as bishop in 1811 at age 36, he thought nothing of traveling 2,000 miles on horseback to make his winter visits. In the summer he often logged 4,000 miles. He founded Hobart College in Geneva, New York, and General Theological Seminary in New York City.

During his 19-year career the number of parishes in his diocese grew from fifty to almost one hundred seventy. The number of clergy grew from twenty-six to one hundred thirty-three. When Bishop Hobart died at age fifty-five he was one of the most beloved figures in New York. Some people thought he could have been elected governor, though many people wondered why this work-aholic hadn't died sooner.

However, the most formative influences on our church didn't come from any one personality or event. They came from two evolving movements that continue to shape us today: the Evangelical Movement and the Anglo-Catholic Movement. They developed almost a century apart, but their convictions and characteristics help us understand how the Lord continues to form Episcopalians today.

Bishop John Henry Hobart

In addition to his tireless ministry to Episcopal parishes, Bishop Hobart strongly supported work among the Oneida Indians.

Evangelicals

Anyone who's ever gone away to college knows what a life-changing experience it is.

This was the case for young two brothers from a small town in England who went away to Oxford University in the early 18th century.

John and Charles Wesley were the sons of an Anglican priest.

William Wilberforce
(1759-1883)

The Evangelical William Wilberforce led the campaign to end slavery in Britain. Fueled by his conversion in 1789 he became the leading abolitionist voice in Parliament. He believed slavery was a sin and often quoted Scripture and biblical ideas of justice in his speeches. He is regarded as one of Britian's greatest social reformers

They were raised in a pious home, devoted to prayer and helping the poor. Mature beyond their years, they took their religion very seriously.

When they got to Oxford, the Wesleys surrounded themselves with like-minded Christians. They founded 'The Holy Club.' They were known for their piety and strict devotion. Members were also known for their particular 'method' of studying the Bible (later followers became known as Methodists).

Following college, in 1728, John Wesley became a Church of England priest while Charles concentrated on writing church music.

Charles would compose no fewer than 6,000 hymns, including 'Hark, the Herald Angels Sing!' Many people think he was the greatest hymn writer of all time.

During their ministries, the Wesleys went through profound, though separate, conversion experiences, which led them to pray more, become more generous and preach the Gospel whenever they could.

Soon they joined the great revivalist and evangelical Anglican priest, George Whitefield. All three spent several years in Georgia. They played significant roles in the movement known as the 'Great Awakening.' They preached emotional sermons on the depravity of humanity and the saving power of the cross. The Wesleys helped fuel a wave of evangelical fervor and influence felt throughout the United States. The Wesleys saw their 'Methodism' as a renewal movement within the bounds of the Church of England. However, subsequent Anglican leadership decided to sever ties.

The Wesleys significantly influenced both the Church of England and the Episcopal Church. The Evangelical Movement they started was based on personal piety, evangelical outreach, emphasis on the poor, the vastness of God's love, and the importance of an adult conversion experience. The Wesleys helped revive a church mired in Deism.

They helped us return to a New Testament model of vibrancy and energetic expectation of Christ's kingdom. Their sincere and straightforward understanding of the Gospel continues to challenge us. Evangelical Episcopalians remind us of the importance of personal purpose and mission. They inspire fresh conversations over crucial issues facing the church.

Anglo-Catholics

You could call it opposition. You could call it reaction.

John Henry Newman

Episcopalians thank Tracterians like Newman for emphasizing traditions that are still with us today, like weekly Communion. Newman was such a strong proponent of Catholic practice that he left the Church of Eng-land after 20 years of ministry. He joined the Roman Catholic Church where he distinguished himself as a scholar and earned the title 'Cardinal.'

But one hundred years later, a second renewal movement swept through our church. This one was aimed at recapturing the tradition, history, Sacraments and symbols of the ancient Church.

The Anglo-Catholic Movement (sometimes called the Oxford Movement) also began on the campus of Oxford University and it started when several scholars published little booklets or 'tracts.' These 'Tracterians' urged us to look back and recapture pre-Reformation Catholic practices and traditions of which we were once a part.

From 1833 through 1841 notable Anglicans like John Keble, Edward Pusey and John Henry Newman published a total of ninety 'Tracts for the Times'. Many were about the Holy Eucharist and urged an overhaul of its place in church services. Tracterians pushed for formal and even elaborate ritual. They reminded us of the importance of our Christian symbols—altar candles, incense, Eucharistic vestments and linens. They emphasized the role of mystery and imagination. They promoted our church's return to an ancient and neglected sense of reverence and holiness.

The Oxford Movement spread to the United States later in the century and became particularly popular in many Midwestern cities.

However, not everyone jumped on the bandwagon. Critics called Anglo-Catholics 'Papists' and 'Romish.' They charged them with tossing out the main principles of the Reformation.

Anglo-Catholics became known for their work of building new relationships with other Christians. Anglo-Catholic Episcopalians initiated conversations with Roman Catholics, Orthodox Christians, and Protestants. A fresh, new search for Christ amidst all of Christ's Church was born.

Anglo-Catholics also emphasized scholarship. Their academic work helped form the framework of the 1928 and 1979 Prayer Books.

And Anglo-Catholics placed great importance on Christ's presence in the gathered community. They have given us a fresh understanding of our genuine interdependence.

In these two broad movements, we continue to see how the Holy Spirit speaks through all of us—even those with whom we may disagree. We've benefited to no end from the points of view represented by Evangelicals, Anglo-Catholics and everybody in between. God's Church needs all of its members. As St. Paul wrote, "The eye cannot say to the hand, 'I have no need of you,' nor again the head to the feet, 'I have no need of you.'" (1 Corinthians 12:20)

Together

As the Episcopal Church moved into the twentieth Century we invested a lot of time and energy into working with other Christians. We really wanted to help bring different churches together. We still do.

Anglicans consider ourselves both Catholic (in that we trace our origins to the first disciples and cherish our sacramental history) and Reformed (in that we hold to the formative convictions of the Reformers, especially the primacy of Scripture as the supreme authority in establishing Christian doctrine). Thus, we have always seen ourselves as uniquely equipped to broker helpful dialog between Christians of many different traditions.

In 1886, the House of Bishops adopted the Chicago Lambeth Quadrilateral. It outlined four core convictions (see page 876 in the Book of Common Prayer).

The document helped bring Christians from many different traditions to new levels of trust and personal relationships. This played a big part in the founding of the National Cathedral in Washington, D.C. at the beginning of the twentieth century.

"A National House of Prayer for All People"

RMESKILL

The National Cathedral in Washington, D.C. embodies, in bricks and mortar, the Episcopal Church's profound commitment to the work of unity. It has been the site of some of the most important religious events in the nation, like the President's Inaugural Prayer Service and the National Prayer and Remembrance service following 9/11. Its beauty and grandeur draw hundreds of thousands of visitors each year.
(www.nationalcathedral.org)

Our work for unity has continued:

- In 1910, Bishop Charles Brent initiated steps that led to the founding of the World Council of Churches.

- In 1927 the Episcopal Church took part in the first World Faith and Order Conference in Lausanne, Switzerland.
- In 1962 the Consultation on Church Union was established to bring greater unity among several of America's big Protestant churches.
- In 2000 Episcopalians and Lutherans signed a historic agreement. We approved 'Called to Common Mission.' Now our clergy share ministries like never before.
- In 2006 Episcopalians joined dozens of the largest churches in the world to form Christian Churches Together (www.christianchurchestogether.org), which has launched an important campaign against poverty.
- Today the Episcopal Church has commissions regularly engaging in dialog with Presbyterians, Roman Catholics, Pentecostals and others.

Of course we're not the only Christians who'd love to bring Christ's church closer together.

And we're happy to see more people try.

Jesus once prayed, "I ask... on behalf of those who will believe in me through their word, that they may all be one." (John 17:20-21)

Just imagine if this were true!

Just imagine if we could actually heed this prayer.

What would the world be like if all Christians worked together?

It is a heavenly vision that continues to inspire Episcopalians, and many other Christians, to endlessly reach out to those with whom we may not agree.

It is vital work given the temperament of our modern world. And it is the Lord's work. It isn't just crucial for ourselves—it is integral to the peace and safety of the world—and to helping the next generation who we are in charge of showing the ropes.

12. PROPHET

Learning from the Past?

Prophet

I once worked for a prophet. Really. She fit your typical unassuming prophet's M.O. She was short, she was thin, and she… was a she. As far as I know, no one ever passed her on the street and said, 'Now there's a prophet!' Years ago she got angry at the injustice in our city. Homelessness was on the rise. Kids were getting arrested for shootings. Minorities weren't getting good jobs. Businesses were moving out. Schools were losing good teachers. Our community was hurting. Something needed to be done.

We needed a prophet.

So into this sad and depressing situation, the Lord sent us one. And just to show God has a sense of humor, the Lord chose a prophet named Joy.

Joy answered the call and soon joined a small group of like-minded people. They formed a community-organizing group.

Before she knew it there were more than twenty churches, charities and other organizations coming together for the same reasons.

At the group's first big rally, she told a crowd of 800 people that she was tired of the injustice and the oppression. She told them that God was tired too. Prophets have always been clamorous and a bit edgy. As one writer puts it, "The prophet Deborah wouldn't have beaten the tar out of the Canaanites by issuing directives from her living room any more than Moses would have gotten his people out of Egypt by writing letters to the New York Times."[2]

Joy challenged us to work for justice. If we all stood together and worked for change, a bit of God's world could come to our world. It did. And it will.

Joy is one of many contemporary prophets who are being called to speak out against the injustices of our day. By 'prophet' I

4) Be a minister, regardless of whether or not you wear a collar.

5) Plant a native tree. There is theological significance in planting a seed and watching it grow into something that will stand long after you are gone.

6) Look beyond the soup kitchen. The church's tried-and-true methods of hospitality are important, but think of how you and those closest to you can transform society, making soup kitchens unnecessary.

7) Reconcile. Contact estranged relatives and slighted prom dates. Before Jesus comes back, begin the work of forgiveness by offering it to others and receiving it yourself.

8) Watch a movie. Specifically, create a community event around mindful documentaries. Challenge attendees to change one thing about the way they live their lives for the sake of future generations.

9) Tithe. No, seriously. It's an ancient Christian practice that can transform your sense of community and ideas of what really belongs to God.

10) Join life. Pray ceaselessly. Go skinny-dipping. Sing boldly in the shower and in church. Waiting for the Second Coming shouldn't be about cowering in fear of a terrifying future. If we love God, we trust God. Enjoy one another in the world, while we're here. Life speeds by unless we catch it in meaningful moments.[1]

Prophet

The Episcopal Church made history in 1794 when we helped establish the first black church in Philadelphia and one of the first in the country.

In 1786 white members of St. George's Methodist Episcopal Church decided black members should sit in the balcony. So the Rev. Absalom Jones, his friend Richard Allen and the other black members walked out.

William White, Bishop of Philadelphia, agreed to accept the group as an Episcopal parish. The African Episcopal Church of St. Thomas opened on July 17, 1794. In 1802 Jones was ordained priest and served as the parish's rector. He was the first black priest in the Episcopal Church. Today about 5% of Episcopalians are African-American and 8% of our bishops are.

mean a wise person who senses the future direction of events then boldly calls to account the powers that be. Prophets understand the place of social justice in the Jewish and Christian traditions.

The voice of the prophet can be heard throughout the Bible. There's Isaiah, Jeremiah, John the Baptist, Jesus, and Paul.

Down through history devout Christians like William Wilberforce, Sojourner Truth, and Martin Luther King, Jr. have been moved by the Holy Spirit to work on behalf of the oppressed to bring about positive social change.

Times have changed, but the prophet's role stays the same: speak truth to power—speak justice to oppression.

Countless people have done this. Countless churches have done this.

Including mine.

Episcopalians make promises at their baptisms to, "strive for justice and peace among all people and respect the dignity of every human being."

We try our very best to live this out. A lot of other churches do too.

Sure, we've taken our hits (prophets always do). But we think it's God's work—so we try so hard to make it our work.

New Thing

Like most churches, my church entered the 20th century barring women from any substantial leadership positions. Young girls could not expect to be acolytes or grow up to be lectors or lay preachers, much less priests. There were 'deaconesses,' established in 1889, but women couldn't go any further. While male deacons could become priests or bishops, deaconesses were… well, just deaconesses.

Our church had been talking about women's rights for years, especially in the 1920's during the Suffragette movement. Then, during the Civil Rights era, the issue became more important. "The evil of antifeminism (Jane Crow) [is] identical to the evil of racism (Jim Crow)" said an activist Episcopal lawyer in 1965. We began to see the similarities between the two.

In 1970, women were recognized as deputies to General Convention for the first time. Convention voted to eliminate the distinction between deaconesses and deacons. This took away the main theological barrier for women to become priests.

This was an extraordinary move.

In our church's entire history we had never had women priests.

Could God be calling us to do a new thing?

We listened, we studied, we prayed and we waited.

However, some of us just couldn't hold off. On July 29, 1974, in a well-orchestrated and highly irregular ceremony in Philadelphia, three bishops took matters into their own hands. They consecrated 11 female deacons as priests—without the approval of the larger church.

We were being pushed by our prophets—or were we?

These were unsanctioned consecrations and they sent shock waves through the Church. It served as a catalyst for the next General Conven-

Katharine Jefferts Schori

HERB GUNN

In 2006, the Right Reverend Katharine Jefferts Schori, bishop of Nevada, was elected Presiding Bishop of the Episcopal Church . She became the first female head of our church and the first female in the Anglican Communion to become a Primate (I know, it's an unfortunate title but it simply means the chief bishop of a province). Jefferts Schori is a scientist by background and when not tending to the flock, she likes to fly planes.

tion. In 1976 we debated, we prayed, then we voted for women to be eligible to serve in all three orders of ministry; as deacons, priests and bishops. We joined other provinces and diocese of the Anglican Communion (Hong Kong 1971 and Canada later in 1976) and since then the Church of England (1994) now ordains women as priests.

This vote turned out to be a very good move.

Just ask anybody who's gotten to know female clergy.

Today more than one quarter of our clergy are women (not bad, seeing as women make up 58% of our church).[2] They're not only growing in number, but in power.

In 1989, Barbara Harris became the first of many women to be consecrated bishop. In 2006, Katharine Jefferts Schori, Bishop of Nevada, became the first woman ever elected as Presiding Bishop, the leader of the Episcopal Church.

Decades after these first ordinations, we're still thanking God for the ministry of female clergy. We believe we've re-discovered a sense of what St. Paul was getting at when he wrote, "There is no longer Jew or Greek, there is no longer slave or free, there is no longer male and female; for all of you are one in Christ Jesus." (Galatians 3:28)

In the 1970s we made a very tough decision—and it's paid off.

We think we saw God do a new thing.

Newer Thing

At the same time we were reconsidering the role of women, we also began talking more about gays and lesbians in our church. It's an issue society in general was talking about and one that nearly every church is wrestling with today. The same voices calling for civil rights and equality for women were now being heard through the gay liberation movement of the 1970s and 1980s.

Again, we listened.

The first national convention of a group of gay Episcopalians called 'Integrity' was held in Chicago in 1975. Members were loyal Episcopalians who wanted to come to terms with their own sexuality as Christians within the Church and not as pariahs. Listening to the voices of psychologists, biologists, and the Bible convinced them that sexual preference should no longer disqualify them for church leadership. Some Episcopalians were adamantly opposed. They also cited Scripture as well as the church's long-standing tradition of not ordaining homosexuals. We listened to both sides.

Taking a Stand for Gay Rights

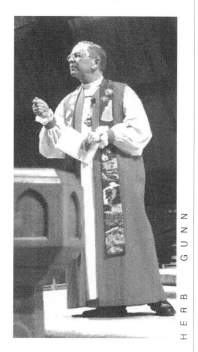

HERB GUNN

Episcopalians took a historic and controversial stand for gay rights in 2003 when The Rev. V. Gene Robinson was ordained bishop (above). Contrary to early critics, his diocese in New Hampshire has experienced growth during his tenure.

In 1976 General Convention declared, "homosexual persons are children of God" who deserve not only pastoral care, but also legal protection in society. Next, the 1979 General Convention differentiated between homosexual orientation (deemed as acceptable) and homosexual activity (deemed as unacceptable). The compromise forbade the ordination of anyone, gay or straight, "engaged in sexual relations outside of marriage."

This did not stop the debate. Some dioceses adopted a "don't ask, don't tell" policy and ordained gays and lesbians. Others outright refused.

The matter finally reached a head in 2003.

After much prayer, study and debate, the Episcopal General Convention voted to approve the ordination of an openly gay priest—The Reverend V. Gene Robinson as the bishop of New Hampshire. He was a 56-year-old divorced father of two who had been living in a committed relationship for 13 years and was much beloved by his constituents. Most Episcopalians believed this difficult road was where the Holy Spirit was leading us. We believed that the broadened acceptance of Christian homosexuals would further open our hearts to the power of honesty, authenticity, understanding, and community, bringing us closer to the inclusive spirit of Jesus Christ.

However many traditional Episcopalians had serious problems with this approval, citing their interpretation of Scripture and tradition.

Several members of the Anglican Communion were upset too.

The Anglican Communion is a worldwide group of forty-four Anglican national churches (more in the next chapter).

The heads of some of these churches voiced disapproval. So the Archbishop of Canterbury directed a committee to study the issue. It led to the release, in 2004, of The Windsor Report. It asked the Episcopal Church to explain its stance on the ordination of gays and lesbians.

Here's part of the answer we gave:

"For almost forty years, members of the Episcopal church have discerned holiness in same-sex relationships and, have come to support the blessing of such unions and the ordination or consecration of persons in those unions. Christian congregations have sought to celebrate and bless same-sex unions because these exclusive, life-long unions of fidelity and care for each other have been experienced as holy. These unions have evidenced the fruit of the Holy Spirit: 'joy, peace, patience, kindness, generosity, faithfulness, gentleness, and self-control.' (Galatians 5:22-25) More specifically, members of our congregations have seen the fruit of such unions as sanctifying human lives by deepening mutual love and by drawing persons together in fidelity and in service to the world."[3]

A vocal minority of our congregations and dioceses remain upset. Talks of schism and re-alignment will probably be with us for some time. We realize our membership in the Anglican Communion may be redefined or even rescinded.

But it's our prayer that a spirit of unity, collegiality and humility will win out. We believe God is leading us through this season. We believe God has opened our hearts to a new love and understanding of inclusivity.

We believe God has shown us a new thing. Our decisiveness on this issue is actually a gift to the next generation of Christians who, polls say, tend to place much less importance on this issue.

Those before us have made a fair amount of progress here. Most other churches aren't nearly as far along. And these issues aren't going away. Our progress means we can now concentrate on other things—the more weighty matters of poverty, AIDS and injustice. As St. Paul once wrote; "this one thing I do… I press on toward the goal for the prize of the heavenly call of God in Christ Jesus." (Philippians 3:13-14) And these words are a call to action.

Action

My friends Marty and Sarah love coffee. One day they sent me an e-mail asking me what kind of coffee the church used. I checked the brand and got back with them. They told me it was not 'fair trade' coffee. They explained that 'fair trade' coffee considers the livelihood of the growers and the environment where the coffee is grown.

Before I knew it, the parish was using 'fair trade' coffee. Before I knew it, Marty and Sarah were spreading the news, leading seminars and teaching parishioners that buying fair trade coffee helps coffee farmers in developing countries use environmentally friendly growing policies as well as receive a fair wage for their harvest.

God's prophetic voice isn't always a dramatic one.

Marty and Sarah, in their calm and gentle manner, had a way of opening our community's eyes to new ways of doing justice. They've helped us talk about not just coffee, but also water pollution and global warming. They have helped us put our faith into action. We believe this is what Christ calls us to do. This is what my church believes more of us should do.

That's why the Episcopal Church funds an international peace and justice ministry based in New York. We also have an Office of Government Relations in Washington, D.C.

We believe the Gospel calls us to advocacy. As former Presiding Bishop Frank Griswold puts it, "Our religious voice in the public square is a staple of who we are. We cannot be unaware of the world around us. Unawareness is a form of self-protection and it is also a form of bondage. It keeps us safe within the prison of our biases and judgments all the while convincing us that we possess the truth."[5]

The Office of Government Relations and the Episcopal Public Policy Network (www.er-d.org/eppn.htm) bring the positions of our Church to our nation's lawmakers. We represent the social policies established by General Convention and Executive Council, including issues of international peace and justice, civil rights, abortion, the environment, racism, war, children's issues, and many more.

Today we're hard at work on the United Nation's Millennium Development Goals (page 14). These are tangible objectives aimed at ending poverty and fighting disease.

Today's prophets are pointing us to malnourished babies, AIDS-infected moms and laid-off factory workers.

Taking Action: Poverty

Episcopalians for Global Reconciliation help to make the MDGs a bigger part of our lives:

www.e4gr.org

These are the voices we're hearing. These are the voices we think everybody should hear.

That's why today, more than ever, we need more prophets.

13. CONNECT

I am because we are.
We are because He is.

Kenyan Eucharistic Liturgy

Members of the Anglican Communion:

- The Anglican Church in Aotearoa, New Zealand & Polynesia
- The Anglican Church of Australia
- The Church of Bangladesh
- Igreja Episcopal Anglicana do Brasil
- The Anglican Church of Burundi
- The Anglican Church of Canada
- The Church of the Province of Central Africa
- Iglesia Anglicana de la Region Central de America
- Province de L'Eglise Anglicane Du Congo
- The Church of England
- Hong Kong Sheng Kung Hui
- The Church of the Province of the Indian Ocean
- The Church of Ireland
- The Nippon Sei Ko Kai (The Anglican Communion in Japan)
- The Episcopal Church in Jerusalem & The Middle East
- The Anglican Church of Kenya
- The Anglican Church of Korea
- The Church of the Province of Melanesia
- La Iglesia Anglicana de Mexico
- The Church of the Province of Myanmar (Burma)
- The Church of Nigeria
- The Church of North India (United)
- The Church of Pakistan (United)
- The Anglican Church of Papua New Guinea
- The Episcopal Church in the Philippines
- L'Eglise Episcopal au Rwanda
- The Scottish Episcopal Church
- Church of the Province of South East Asia
- The Church of South India (United)
- The Church of the Province of Southern Africa
- Iglesia Anglicana del Cono Sur de America
- The Episcopal Church of the Sudan
- The Anglican Church of Tanzania
- The Church of the Province of Uganda
- The Episcopal Church in the USA
- The Church in Wales
- The Church of the Province of West Africa
- The Church in the Province of the West Indies

These are designated Extra-Provincial:

- The Church of Ceylon
- Iglesia Episcopal de Cuba
- Bermuda
- The Lusitanian Church
- The Reformed Episcopal Church of Spain
- Falkland Islands

Connect

I remember waking up to the sound of mullahs calling the faithful to worship. I quickly showered, got dressed, and met my driver in the lobby.

The bright sun was well over the horizon as we made our way through a tightly woven maze of city streets.

We kicked up clouds of dust as we passed sandaled Pakistanis walking to work. The smell of unfamiliar breakfasts filled the air. Exotic music blared from the dash. The speakers were shot.

Soon we arrived. As I walked in someone handed me a bulletin and book. I was at Holy Trinity Anglican Church in Dubai. I was in foreign place.

But quite suddenly, I was very much at home.

If you've ever traveled very far you know how comforting it is to find the familiar amidst the foreign. Finding commonalities with people who are vastly different can be a major challenge. It helps if you have connections —like a whole church full of people who speak the same language.

Spokes

Episcopalians trace our heritage in two directions. We go vertically back to St. Peter. And we go horizontally—to our relationships with millions of other Anglicans all over the world. Together we make up a unique association called the Anglican Communion.

We're the third largest collection of Christians in the world (after Roman Catholics and Eastern Orthodox).

There are more than eighty million of us, and we're growing.

The Anglican Communion is made up of forty-four national and regional church associations in one hundred and sixty countries worldwide. This includes more than five hundred dioceses spread over every continent.

Our Communion has developed in stages over the last few hundred years, so the organization is relatively new. What holds us together isn't a formal legal structure or the authority of some church hierarchy. It's a shared conviction and participation in the basic ideas of the English Reformation—namely, Episcopal government by apostolic succession, liturgical worship, and the Bible informed and interpreted by tradition, reason and the creeds as our main source of doctrine.

We consider the Archbishop of Canterbury our spiritual leader. But compared to others like the Pope, the Archbishop's role is limited. He makes no claims to infallibility and he's not allowed to hand down laws that members are legally bound to obey. Rather, the Archbishop of Canterbury, as the head of the Church of England, is understood as the symbolic head of the Communion. He is the 'primus inter pares,' first among equals. While he serves as our spokesman, he doesn't have any formal authority outside of England. He doesn't make rules as much as he makes very savvy suggestions.

This gives a lot of leeway to member churches. Each national church pretty much rules itself and is free to figure out specific answers to questions about doctrine and organization.

What we mean by communion is that church services, liturgies and ceremonies conducted in one parish are officially recognized in others. When I visit an Anglican church in another country the similarities are clear. Like Holy Trinity, Dubai, the service is similar to the service I attend back home.

Communion also describes the relationship between the Archbishop of Canterbury and its member churches.

Think of a wagon wheel. The Archbishop of Canterbury is at the hub. Each spoke leads out from the center and ends at a church. To be a member of the Anglican Communion means to be in communion with the Archbishop—to be a spoke in the wheel.

Relationships with other members don't play out the same way. For example, when the Episcopal Church made decisions about women and gays in ministry other members of the Communion objected, but our framework meant there was little they could do. This doesn't mean our framework will never change. It may, very soon.

However if re-alignments and re-configurations arise it won't be the first time. Or the last. Keeping churches connected remains a tough job. But we'll continue to work hard at it. As Archbishop Desmond Tutu once said, "Yes, the Anglican Communion is quite messy, but it's just so loveable."

Structure

Keeping connected at the local level is an important job too. Like other churches, we have our own way of organizing ourselves. We have our own way of forming communities that comes out of a time-tested and uniquely American structure.

You might remember that many of the founding members of the Episcopal Church were also key players, even authors in creating the U.S. Constitution. It's no accident that the structure of our Church mirrors the U.S. government's.

You might also remember that the word 'Episcopal' comes from the Greek word for bishop. In our church, bishops are really important. While Presbyterian churches are run by presbyters (elders) and Congregational churches are run by congregations, Episcopal churches are governed to a great degree by bishops—albeit with a strong (and limiting) strain of democracy.

The Episcopal Church does its major business every three years. That's when our two houses, the House of Deputies and the House of Bishops, meet in General Convention.

This is similar to the U.S. Congress. The House of Deputies loosely corresponds to the House of Representatives and the House of Bishops, to the Senate. The House of Deputies is made up of delegates sent from each diocese, which sends four lay people (non-clergy) and four clergy. The House of Bishops is made up of bishops from each of the 100 dioceses in the church.

One Way to Look at It:

General Convention	=	Congress
House of Bishops	=	Senate
House of Deputies	=	House of Representatives
Presiding Bishop	=	President
Executive Council	=	Cabinet
Dioceses	=	States, or regions therein
Diocesan Conventions	=	State Legislature
Bishops	=	Governors
Deaneries	=	Counties
Parishes	=	Cities
Vestries	=	Town Council
Rectors	=	Mayors

While the diocesan bishop is the head of a diocese, some dioceses may have assisting bishops. There are also a fair number of retired bishops. In fact, there are over 300 bishops in the Episcopal Church, and about half of them are retired.

Every nine years these bishops elect a Presiding Bishop, the 'PB.' Think of the PB as our elected 'president,' or at least our spokesperson.

The PB's cathedral is the National Cathedral in Washington, D.C. The PB lives at the Episcopal Church Center at 815 Second Avenue in New York (tell the cabbie one block from the United Nations on the east side of mid-Manhattan). This is also the headquarters of the Episcopal Church, nicknames "815."

A smaller version of the national church is the local diocese. A diocese is a group of churches in a specific geographic area. Just like General Convention, each diocese meets in its own convention. Every year clergy and lay delegates elected from each parish come to conduct their business.

Most dioceses also have deaneries, or smaller groups of churches, organized by geographic region—a smaller group makes it easier to meet more frequently.

The parish is the smallest level of government. There are more than 7,200 parishes in the Episcopal Church.

Like other churches, Episcopalians have their own code words. We don't have janitors. We have sextons. Our parishes don't have basements. We have undercrofts. And we don't have pastors. We have rectors.

Although some parishes may have a vicar or a priest-in-charge, a rector heads most Episcopal parishes. Rectors are not simply appointed by the bishop. Rectors are 'called,' or hired by a parish after a search process. Candidates from all over the country often apply. It usually takes about a year to hire a new rector once the previous one has left. Finalists are extensively interviewed and go through background checks. Once chosen, the rector may hire ordained assistants sometimes called curates or associate rectors, who report to the rector, not the parish.

Each year the parish holds its Annual Meeting. This is similar to diocesan convention. This is where the parish paperwork gets done. We approve a budget. We also elect (or approve) the parish's governing board. This board is called (another code word) the vestry.

The vestry is the legal entity of the parish with regard to all parish property. It's usually made up of twelve people. It usually meets monthly. The vestry's job is, "to help define and articulate the mission of the congregation; to support the church's mission by word and deed, to select the rector, to ensure effective organization and planning, and to manage resources and finances."[1]

Vestries have a senior warden, who leads the parish in between rectors and supports the rector when there's one in place. Another leader, called a junior warden, is usually in charge of grounds and property.

Other vestry members often take liaison roles within the parish to help the vestry keep tabs on what's going on.

Our structures aren't always efficient. Sometimes they do more harm than good. But on the whole, they're pretty effective ways to help us do the work we're called to do—a big part of which is mission.

Mission

I have some friends named Bob and Shirley. They're retired. They love to travel. One day they came to my office and said they wanted to go on a special trip. They wanted to go on a mission trip.

Very soon we were in contact with the diocese of Haiti. Very soon Bob and Shirley were traveling to Port au Prince. Very soon Bob and Shirley had inspired a five-year partnership between our parish and the Church of the Ascension in the town of Thor, Haiti.

Through the friendships Bob and Shirley made, our parish has been able to send textbooks, school supplies, shampoo, medicine, tools and loads of other things to our new friends in Haiti.

In return we receive letters, artwork and maybe one day, a visit. Every Sunday we pray for each other.

> Want to Partner with
> a Third World Parish?
> www.episcopalchurch.org
> /companion.htm

Sign, Sign, Everywhere a Sign

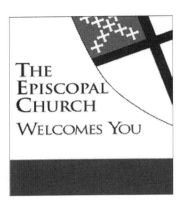

THE EPISCOPAL CHURCH WELCOMES YOU

Ever seen a sign like this?

They are in thousands of cities across the United States. They usually advertise a parish's name and Sunday worship schedule.

Making connections like this is common in my church. World and local missions are supported and encouraged by the Episcopal Church. Permanent, long-term, and short-term mission work is available for qualified candidates, check out the "Mission" link at www.epis-copalchurch.org.

Our partnerships with parishes inside the United States are also valuable. Neighboring parishes often co-sponsor youth and adult education programs. Parishes frequently welcome pilgrims and youth workers from far-away congregations who need housing or other resources.

Our familiar red, white and blue sign has a mission all its own. It has welcomed many an out of town guest looking for a Sunday worship service. Chances are there's at least one in your town.

Our shared tradition, nationally and internationally, offers us a world of resources and opportunities, which uniquely equips us for the challenging work ahead – we stand in awe and thanksgiving of these God-given connections.

Feed the World and Build Your Vocabulary

www.freerice.com helps feed the world vis-à-vis a never-ending vocabulary quiz. For each correct answer 20 grains of rice is donated to fight world hunger (the site makes money from advertisements). It may not sound like a lot but wait 'til you kill an hour playing it.

14. REFUGE

"[The Episcopal faith] is one religion where laughing
at our own absurdities is a basic spiritual discipline
and we're invited to rejoice in how much we have still to learn
of God instead of how much we know."

L William Countryman

Refuge

Every once in a while somebody asks why the doors of our church are painted red.

Depending on my mood, the response may include a reference to red as a symbol of refuge rooted in the Old Testament (Numbers 35:9-15) 'right of sanctuary' given to the perpetrators of manslaughter.

Or the answer may refer to a more distant history, and ancient Egypt where most everybody believed that sacred spaces held sacred objects. Those fleeing violence often high-tailed it into the temples of Osiris and Amon knowing that their pursuers believe it to be sacrilege to remove a person from such a sacred place.

Or a lofty pontification might emerge about King Ethelbert's English law (circa 600 AD) that gave the right of asylum to fleeing suspects when they entered churches.

Of course, sometimes I just say there was a sale on red paint.

Many Episcopal churches paint their doors red because,

like most churches, we consider our parishes to be places of refuge. Red is the color of Christ's blood, the sacrifice of the martyrs, the power of the Holy Spirit, and the holy ground that lies beyond our red doors. It's an important reminder to members, but an even more profound message for our visitors.

We are a safe place.

We are a peaceful place.

We are a place of refuge.

Visit

So you're thinking about walking through those red doors and actually trying out an Episcopal church?

I've been there.

I know it can be scary—especially if you don't know a soul in the parish. But don't worry, Episcopalians, for the most part don't bite (hard).

In fact, most of us tend to be introverts, even shy.

This means that behind the formality and reverence found in many parishes you usually find the warmest, most generous-hearted people on the face of the planet. Remember,

Narthex: It's the enclosed space at the entrance of the nave of a church.

Nave: This is the main part of a church where the congregation sits. It's from an old word for ship—in older churches the beams of the roof resembled the beams and timbers in the sides of a ship.

Sacristy: This is the room near the altar where priests dress for the service. It's also the room where the communion vessels and vestments are kept.

Sanctuary: This is the part of a church immediately around the altar. Sometimes it's used to refer to the whole interior of the church, but this isn't the usual Episcopal usage.

Senior Warden: This is the primary congregational lay leader.

Sexton: The Sexton is commonly head of maintenance and custodial services and may perform additional duties such as ringing the church bell.

Vestry: This is the governing board of a local Episcopal parish consisting of lay members. The group usually makes basic decisions about the parish budget, building plans, etc. Usually headed by a senior warden and assisted by a junior warden who often follows the senior warden in office.

815: This is the short reference to the main office complex of the Episcopal Church in New York: Episcopal Church Center, 815 Second Avenue, New York, NY 10017, (800)-334-7626. [2]

most Episcopalians are converts and were probably visitors once just like you. Since most Episcopal parishes are small to medium sized, you will not go unnoticed for long. You will find yourself sitting next to people who are looking for authentic community, people who will save a seat for you when you arrive and miss you when you are not there.

When visiting an Episcopal parish for the first time, double-check the worship schedule. Lots of parishes change worship times from summer to winter, during the holidays, and for special programs—so call ahead.

When the big day comes, get there early, pick up a bulletin, and just sit and look at what's going on.

Most parish buildings are awash in symbols.

Paintings, sculptures, stained glass, and lofty spaces can take a lifetime to appreciate. Just like an office or a living room, you can tell a lot about a church by the way it is decorated.

You also have time to familiarize yourself with the order of service.

You may want to take some books down from the rack in the pew in front of you—The Book of Common Prayer and the Hymnal 1982, or some other music book.

During the course of the service you'll find yourself standing, sitting or kneeling. Standing is something we do to show respect. We stand to sing, to hear the Gospel, to say the Creed and some congregations stand to pray just like the Jews in Jesus' day probably did. Some people stand while the priest prays the Eucharistic prayer.

Sitting means we're ready to learn. We sit to listen to the Old and New Testament lessons as well as the Psalm and the sermon.

Kneeling is a way we show reverence (we remember that the Lord Almighty is here—and that's driven a lot of people to their knees). We kneel to confess our sins, to receive absolution and to pray (although standing for prayer is an ancient and acceptable posture).

Also, some people genuflect (briefly kneel on one knee) or bow. Some people make the sign of the cross. Some people kneel when others are standing. These are personal acts of piety and are completely optional.

If it's for you, fine, join in. If not, don't.

The ancient and sacred nature of such 'body prayers' is always respected, and I like to think most people have better things to do than keep track of other people's pieties.

About halfway through the service the choir or a soloist may sing. It's called an anthem. It's a musical piece offered to God. We watch and enjoy. But don't be surprised if nobody claps when it's over. We look at anthems foremost as offerings to God, not entertainment for a crowd. We don't clap when we finish a hymn either. Of course you can clap if you want—but you've been warned.

Toward the end of the service it'll come time to take Holy Communion.
In every Episcopal parish everybody's welcome to come forward.

Yes, We Use Real Wine...

Scripture and the vast majority of church historians tell us Jesus used real wine. So we do. Once consecrated, we believe Christ is equally present in both the bread and the wine. So if a recovering alcoholic only wants bread that's OK, Christ is there. And if someone has a wheat allergy and only drinks the wine, that's OK too, Christ is equally present.

...And Yes, It Is Safe.

Canadian cardiologist David Gould has done extensive research on the spread of disease from sharing a common communion cup. A recent report says churchgoers are more likely to get sick from airborne infections than from sharing a chalice. Most communion wine is fortified, which means it has a very high alcohol content - this kills germs. "If communion cups were a danger," Gould says, "there would be cases of mass infections." And there aren't. Cheers.[3]

If you're a baptized Christian you're free to receive communion.

If you haven't been baptized or don't want communion, come on up anyway, just cross your arms over your chest and the priest will bless you.

If you're going to take communion most parishes expect you to stretch your arms forward, open-palm, one hand over the other to receive the bread. You may hear the words, "Body of Christ." The proper response is "Amen" to 'I'm four years old!').

Communion bread can take many forms. Some parishes use homemade pita bread. Others use pre-pressed, unleavened wafers (some say it's easier to believe Christ rose from the dead than to believe these skinny little wafers are actually bread—but they are). When the chalice comes around, you're free to dip your bread in the wine (the official $10 vocabulary word is intinction). Or you can take a sip of wine. The person with the chalice will extend the cup toward you and expect you to guide it to your lips, but usually won't expect you to take it outright.

Once you get back to your seat don't be surprised if you see people kneeling in prayer. Following the Post Communion prayer, blessing and dismissal, there is usually a final hymn. Except on very rare occasion, no one leaves the church until the final hymn is finished.

At this point you're free to go. However—you may have been invited (verbally or in the bulletin) to an after-church activity peculiar to Episcopal churches. It's called Coffee Hour.

Episcopalians absolutely love their Sunday morning coffee—some call it our third sacrament.

The event usually takes place in a nearby lounge or parish hall, which may or may not be easy to find. In fact, you may or may not be properly greeted. One big reason is because Coffee Hour is an important social hour for us. Since most Episcopal churches are small, we consider this our weekly 'family reunion.' We get to see people we know and love. We get to see people we only see at church. Unfortunately, an unrecognized face can be overlooked.

So here's a tip: take the initiative and introduce yourself if you have to. Your courage can be handsomely rewarded with new friends. Like families, parishes can take time to break into, but once you do, the payoff is usually worth more than the effort.

Hatch, Match and Dispatch

One of the ways God brings people into my church is through life passage events, like baptisms, weddings and funerals.

Most parishes consider it an honor to participate in these. Sure, we have guidelines. They're meant to help people understand the meanings and boundaries of these sacred rites. Some parishes ask people to become members first, others don't. A parish near you would have specific answers. Joining an Episcopal Church is mostly about showing up. It's been said that Christian initiation is 10% indoctrination and 90% incorporation. Depending on whether or not you have been baptized, this means that a short class or a meeting with the rector may be all that is required.

The real work of membership is done as you become part of the parish, participating in regular worship, living into the life of the church.

It all starts with baptism.

Episcopalians baptize adults and babies.

Our prayer book tells us, "Holy Baptism is full initiation by water and the Holy Spirit into Christ's Body, the Church." (BCP 299) For adults, baptism is an adult declaration of the Lordship of Christ in one's life. For children, through the promises of parents and godparents, it signifies their sharing of citizenship in the covenant, membership in Christ, and redemption by God.

The Outline of the Faith, or Catechism (found in the back of the prayer book) explains it this way, "Promises are made for them by their parents and sponsors, who guarantee that the infants will be brought up within the church, to know Christ, and be able to follow him. (BCP 859)"

Everybody who gets baptized has at least one person, preferably two, who serve as sponsors. If the candidate is a baby these folk are commonly called godparents. They may or may not be Episcopalians, but they should be Christians.

And they have to be willing to follow through on the pledges they make. The baby's parents commonly join the godparents in this ceremony. Gifts like prayer books, Bibles or jewelry are appropriate. As the youngster grows, some godparents send baptismal anniversary cards to remind the child of their commitment to Christ through their baptism.

Once somebody's baptized, in most Episcopal parishes they're free to receive Holy Communion, regardless of their age. For children this is a life-shaping experience that reminds them, from a young age, of these words used in the baptism ceremony; they are 'marked and sealed as Christ's own forever.'

As the child grows older, Episcopalians are expected to seek confirmation. This is a formal occasion to make a public profession of their faith in Christ—the same profession that was made for them at their baptism.

The bishop performs confirmations. The bishop lays hands on candidates and prays for the Holy Spirit. There are sponsors in confirmation, but their role is not the same as godparents. This time the youngster or adult makes an independent declaration of their faith.

If somebody wants to be confirmed in the Episcopal tradition and was baptized in another Christian denomination, that's OK. Episcopalians recognize baptisms in other traditions as long as they were performed with water and in the name of the Trinity (Father, Son and Holy Spirit).

This is also true for people who want to become Episcopalians and have come from other Christian traditions. This is called 'reception' into the Episcopal Church. Again, there's no need to be re-baptized or reconfirmed as long as those rites were performed appropriately in another Christian tradition.

I like to think this is because we recognize faith as a journey that each one of us are on. Rather than attempting to invalidate past experiences, we're much more apt to look for God's hand in them. We use the rites and ceremonies of the church as building blocks upon which God continues to shape our lives.

For many people, marriage is their first contact with an Episcopal church.

Thanks to the striking architecture and movie-set décor of many parishes, some churches find themselves overwhelmed with requests.

Some parishes have to turn couples away simply because they don't have the resources to accommodate them. If you're interested in getting married in an Episcopal church, the best thing to do is to contact the parish and ask about their particular customs.

Episcopalians understand marriage to be a, "solemn and public covenant between a man and a woman in the presence of God." The ministers of the marriage are the man and the woman. The job of the clergy, and everybody who comes, is to witness and to bless.

The Episcopal Church requires that at least the bride or groom be a baptized Christian and at least two other people be present as witnesses. If neither one of the couple is baptized, most parishes are happy to work with them toward baptism before their wedding. Individual states and dioceses may have other requirements. These may include more detailed pre-marital counseling and waiting periods for marriage licenses.

Episcopalians, like many Christians, see weddings as celebrations of God's love.

These celebrations are highly symbolic. They signify, "the

Fit for a Princess

The beauty, elegance and splendor of Anglican liturgy is no more wonderfully observed than at weddings. Lady Diana and Prince Charles showed this to the world when they were wed at St. Paul's Cathedral in London (above).

mystery of the union between Christ and Christ's Church." In the love-struck gazes exchanged by bride and groom we get an idea of how much God loves us. Some parishes also offer a blessing for same-gender couples. Others don't. It is best to check with your local parish to find out.

Funerals are celebrations too, although they don't always feel like it. They're bittersweet. Of course we're sad. Of course we mourn. It's necessary, appropriate and welcomed.

However funerals also stretch us to look at death as the beginning of new life. Finally, we touch the promises of Easter.

The prayer book's liturgies and prayers for funerals are particularly moving and beautiful. I can't tell you how often I've seen them give much-needed relief to the grief and stress that so naturally visit the bereaved.

Episcopalians usually hold funerals inside the church, although we also do them at funeral homes and other places.

Many parishes have a cemetery, special garden or a columbarium where ashes are interred. This is an awesome culmination to a funeral. It reminds us that while the earthly lives of our loved ones have ended, in some mysterious way, they're still with us... talking to us, inspiring us, and reminding us... that the refuge found in God's churches is just a foretaste of the refuge to come.

I wouldn't be surprised if the gates to heaven are painted red.

15. TREASURE

"To my mind there must be, at the bottom of it all,
not an equation, but an utterly simple idea.
And to me that idea, when we finally discover it,
will be so compelling, so inevitable,
that we will say to one another,
'Oh how beautiful. How could it have been otherwise?'"

John Archibald Wheeler

Treasure

Not long ago I was having lunch with a man in my parish who told me how proud he was of his church. He went on about his appreciation for our tradition, liturgy and many of the things we have looked at in the previous chapters. He said, "I'm so happy to belong to a community that thoughtfully deals with the issues of the day."

Then my friend said:
"I think the Episcopal Church is Christianity's buried treasure."

My friend was echoing an optimism that a lot of us have today for our church and our church's future.

Columbia University chaplain Winnie Varghese says, "A recent poll by the Center for American Progress… reported that only four percent of the people polled cited 'abortion or homosexuality' as 'the most serious moral crisis in America today.' …"In the same study, 89% of registered voters polled agreed or strongly agreed that government should uphold the basic decency and dignity of all and take greater steps to help the poor and disadvantaged in America.

"The common prayer of the Episcopal Church is in sync with 89% of the American public!"[1]

And that's a big reason why this book was written.

Most of us want to help fix our broken world. Most of us are looking for places to help us wrestle with our faith—to answer personal questions of meaning and purpose—especially in the context of our work and families. Most of us want places to raise our kids that uphold and instill Christian values. Most of us want to be generous, thoughtful and live faithful lives that spread goodness and peace.

But we have come to realize that we can't do this alone.

We need others. We need communities. We need like-minded Christians who will help us become the kind of people we want to be.

The most popular answer is, and always has been, church.

In fact, religion researcher Robert Wuthnow says church-going rates have not declined since World War II, "Americans are, as they have always been, a religious people—generally not noted for their depth of spirituality, but broadly oriented toward spirituality nonetheless." [2]

Our challenge as 21st century Christians, and our goal as Episcopalians, is to deepen this spirituality. It is not enough for us to simply believe in Christ, but we want to go farther. We want to form ourselves ever deeper into Jesus' disciples—carrying the cross and caring for the world. As we saw in Chapter Two, our culture has put up endless obstacles aimed at keeping us from being the kind of mindful believers we want to be. Preoccupation with 'self' and 'stuff' has crept into every church, chapel and faith community, including mine, making the continual renewal and relevancy of our churches the biggest task North American Christians face.

Our challenge is to find and help build places that help us grow into disciples —to make sense of our spiritual yearnings in the context of our increasingly pluralistic surroundings. Our challenge is to find and help build places that will heal us inwardly so that we might point ourselves outwardly, and play our part, taking full advantage of the amazing opportunities to heal the world that are right in front of us.

Most of us are hesitant to do so by signing up for moral crusades or opting in for theologies that isolate, scare, judge and condemn. In fact, the renewal and re-vitalization of American spirituality will not take place inside these kinds of frameworks—they are too limiting and lack broad appeal. It will take a much more accessible, inclusive and accepting environment. It will take places like the Episcopal Church.

Yes, we are in a period of transition. We are getting our dose of systemic membership decline. Many of our parishes are in desperate need of renewal. But the dust is clearing and a new dawn beckons.

I believe today is exciting time to be an Episcopalian.

As we have seen, our church has a renewed commitment to:
feeding the hungry and clothing the naked;
fighting injustice against the poor and innocent;
standing up for equal rights and the environment;
offering radical hospitality and gritty peacemaking;
making disciples who take Christ, in word and deed, into the world.

Despite the polarizing forces at work in this age of transition, we are solidly emerging as a distinctive and dynamic alternative for many Christians. Our ever-practical Prayer Book outlines an orthodox faith centered on the life and teachings of Jesus. This helps us form sacred, liturgical communities devoted to shaping disciples, raising up holy families and making a difference in the world.

We're about claiming a solid grounding in Jesus Christ rooted in the Bible, ancient tradition and critical thinking. We're about humility and forgiveness, acceptance and inclusion. We're about reasonable compromise, moderation and finding middle ground.

We have made some bold statements and taken some definitive actions in a sincere pursuit of Jesus and the ever-active, ever-wily Holy Spirit.

We care about prayer and we care about justice.
We care less and less about church squabbles.
We care more and more about making this planet a better place.

Now, more than ever, we need the Episcopal Church.

I hope this book helps you understand our journey and see our unique role in the world. I hope this book makes it easier for you to discover how the Episcopal Church may fit into your own spiritual journey. But more than anything, I hope this book helps you see the depth of the Lord's love and faithfulness at work among a desperately flawed though relentlessly determined group of Christians.

It is an active love, endlessly working to renew, restore and revitalize. It is a persistent love that refuses to give up on us, or our churches. And it is an accessible love, embodied in the faithfulness of Christian communities who strive to be the warm smile and open arms of Jesus.

Lifting up this love is the key to any church's renewal. And the more my church does this, the easier I find it to imagine Jesus as an Episcopalian.

Find Out More

The Episcopal Church has an extensive website that can probably answer any question you dream up.

For more information go to:

www.episcopalchurch.org

or

www.comeandgrow.org

ENDNOTES

Chapter 1: Do

[1] Paul Hewson, "Bono's Remarks to the National Prayer Breakfast," February 2, 2006, www.data.org/archives/000774.php

[2] Jeffrey D. Sachs, The End of Poverty: Economic Possibilities for Our Time (New York: Penguin Press, 2005), quoted from news release, www.earth.columbia.edu/news/2005/story03-01-05e.html

[3] Sabina Alkire and Edmund Newell, What Can One Person Do? (New York: Church Publishing, 2005), 78.

[4] Ron Sider, Rich Christians in an Age of Hunger: Moving from Affluence to Generosity, (Nashville: Thomas Nelson Publishing, 1996, fifth edition), 26.

Chapter 2: Transition

[1] Robert B. Reich, "Totally Spent," The New York Times, January 13, 2008, [a signed Op-Ed]

[2] Thomas de Zengotita, Mediated: How the Media Shapes Your World and the Way You Live In It, (New York: Bloomsbury, 2005)

[3] Stephen Prothero, Religious Literacy: What Every American Needs to Know and Doesn't, (San Francisco: HarperCollins, 2007), 30.

[4] Marva Dawn, Reaching Out Without Dumbing Down: A Theology of Worship for this Urgent Time, (Grand Rapids: Eerdmans, 1995), 6-7.

[5] Prothero, 12, 25.

[6] David Kinnaman and Gabe Lyons, UnChristian: What a New Generation Really Thinks About Christianity, (Grand Rapids: Baker, 2007) 11.

[7] Prothero, 36.

[8] Sider, pp. 23-24.

[9] Steve Mullet, quoted passage, Reaching Out Without Dumbing Down: A Theology of Worship for this Urgent Time, (Grand Rapids: Eerdmans, 1995), 228.

[10] Alan Roxburgh, Crossing the Bridge: Church Leadership in a Time of Change, (Rancho Santa Marguerita, CA: Percept Group, 2001), 24.

[11] Shirley Guthrie, "Voices of 2001," Christian Century 2001, www.christiancentury.org

[12] Diana Butler Bass, Christianity for the Rest of Us: How the Neighborhood Church is Transforming the Faith, (San Francisco: Harper, 2006), 36-37.

Chapter 3: Think

[1] Richard Giles, Always Open: Being an Anglican Today, (Cambridge, MA: Cowley), 115.

[2] Donald Armentrout, An Episcopal Dictionary of the Church, (New York: Church Publishing, 2000), 431.

[3] Lawrence N. Crumb, "Anglican Words," The Anglican Digest, vol. 39, no. 6, (Advent, 2007): 21.

[4] John Polkinghorne, Quarks, Chaos and Christianity: Questions to Science and Religion, (New York: Crossroad, 1996), 11-12.

[5] Committee on Science, Technology and Faith of the Executive Council, The Episcopal Church in the United States of America, A Catechism of Creation: An Episcopal Understanding, Part II: Creation and Science, (New York: The Domestic and Foreign Missionary Society of the Protestant Episcopal Church in America, 2005), www.episcopalchurch.org/19021_58398_ENG_HTM.htm

[6] http://www.websterpresby.org/history.asp (accessed June 22, 2008). Also see Tom Hanks' 1998 HBO special From Earth to the Moon.

Chapter 4: Welcome

[1]Cable News Network (CNN), "Ten Commandments Judge Removed from Office," November 14, 2003, www.cnn.com/2003/LAW/11/13/moore.tencommandments (accessed January 2008)

[2]L. William Countryman, Forgiven and Forgiving, (Harrisburg, PA: Morehouse Publishing, 1998), 10.

[3]The Book of Common Prayer, (New York: Church Hymnal Corp., 1979), 336.

Chapter 5: Accept

[1]Dennis Maynard, Those Episkopols, (La Jolla, CA: Dionysus Publications, 1994), 26.

[2]Archbishop Desmond Tutu, "Tutu and Franklin: A Journey Toward Peace," PBS Documentary, (originally aired February 9, 2001). Transcript found at: www.pbs.org/journeytopeace/meettutu/past.html (accessed January 2008)

[3]John Danforth, "Danforth's Challenge to the Episcopal Church," Episcopal News Service, June 17, 2006, www.episcopalchurch.org/75383_75972_ENG_HTM. (accessed January 2008)

Chapter 6: Thank

[1]Dawn, (Wade Roof quoted passage), 132.

[2]Dawn, (Martin Marty quoted passage), 145.

[3] Robert Wuthnow, All in Sync, (University of California Press: Berkeley and Los Angeles, CA, 2003), 76.

[4]Miller McPherson, Lynn Smith-Lovin, Matthew E. Brashears, "Social Isolation in America: Changes in Core Discussion Networks over Two Decades," American Sociological Review, vol. 71, (June, 2006): 353-375.

[5]Rebecca Lyman, Early Christian Traditions (The New Church's Teaching Series, v. 6), (Boston: Cowley, 1999), 65.

[6]Hymn 302, The Hymnal, 1982, (New York: Church Publishing)

[7]Leonel L. Mitchell, Praying Shapes Believing: A Theological Commentary on the Book of Common Prayer, (Harrisburg, PA: Morehouse Publishing, 1985), 181.

[8]George Wayne Smith, Admirable Simplicity: Principles for Worship Planning in the Episcopal Tradition, (New York: Church Publishing, 2001), 95.

Chapter 7: Shape

[1]Lilian Calles Barger, Eve's Revenge: Women and a Spirituality of the Body, (New York: Brazos, 2003), 43-44.

[2]Ibid.

[3] Robert Wuthnow, All In Sync, (University of California Press: Berkeley and Los Angeles, CA, 2003), 28.

[4] Anthony Gottleib, George Barna quoted passage, "Atheists with Attitude," The New Yorker, May 21, 2007: 79.

[5]Resolution A135 asked all of us to adopt Holy Habits, passed by the General Convention of the Episcopal Church, 2003.

Chapter 8: Word

[1]"Built to Last," The New York Times Magazine December 5, 1999: 84. [an article signed Magazine Desk]

[2]Prothero, 30.

[3]Office of Communications, The Episcopal Church Center, To Set Our Hope on Christ: A Response to the Invitation of the Windsor Report, (New York, 2005), 135.

[4]Roger Ferlo, Opening the Bible, (The New Church's Teaching Series, v. 2), (Boston: Cowley, 1997), 4.

[5] Ferlo, (Richard Hooker quoted passage), 5.

[6]Ibid., 6

[7]Ibid., 8.

Chapter 9: Map
[1]Jeffrey Lee, Opening the Prayer Book, (The New Church's Teaching Series, v. 7), (Boston: Cowley, 1999), 7.

[2]Ibid.

[3]Ibid., 9.

[4]Leonel L. Mitchell, Praying Shapes Believing: A Theological Commentary on the Book of Common Prayer, (Harrisburg, PA: Morehouse Publishing, 1985), 2.

[5]Evelyn Underhill and 'The Message of the Wesley's' as quoted by Brennan Manning, The Ragamuffin Gospel, (Sisters, OR: Multnomah, 2000), 13.

Chapter 10: Ancient
[1]Kenneth Scott Latourette, A History of Christianity, Vol. 1, (Harper: San Francisco, 1975), 1-4.

[2]Michael Paulson, "Ma Siss' Place, Part I: Birth," The Boston Globe December 23, 2007, www.boston.com/news/specials/masiss/ (accessed January 2008)

[3]Prothero, 176.

[4]It must be noted that this graph is not to scale. Its purpose is not so much to represent official denominational size as it is to show relationship, affiliation and evolution.

[5]Joseph Buchanan Bernardin, An Introduction to the Episcopal Church, (Harrisburg, PA: Morehouse, 1983), 21.

[6]John R. H. Moorman, A History of the Church in England, (London: Adam and Charles Black, 1976), 3.

[7]Allison Weir, Henry VIII: King and Court, (London: Pimlico, 2002), 124.

Chapter 12: Prophet
[1] Lindsay Lunnum, "10 Things to Do While Waiting for the Second Coming," posted November 8, 2006, www.trinitywallstreet.org/welcome/?article&id=800 (accessed January 2008)

[2] Frederick Buechner, Whistling in the Dark: An ABC Theologized, (New York: HarperOne, 1993), 49.

[3]Louie Crew, "Female Priests in the Episcopal Church," Rutgers University, 2002, http://newark.rutgers.edu/~lcrew/womenpr.html#02 (accessed January 2008)

[4]Office of Communications, The Episcopal Church Center, To Set Our Hope on Christ: A Response to the Invitation of the Windsor Report, (New York, 2005), 8.

[5] Office of Peace and Justice, The Episcopal Church Center, Engage God's Mission: Policy for Action: The Social Policies of the Episcopal Church, U.S.A., (December 2003)

Chapter 14: Connect
[1]Armentrout, 541.

[2]Gerald L. Smith, "Episcopal Things: A Guide for Non-Episcopalians to Many of the Terms and Phrases in use Around Sewanee," 1994, http://smith2.sewanee.edu/glossary/Glossary—Episcopal.html> (accessed January 2008)

[3]Religious News Service, "Dipping Worse than Sipping at Eucharist," The Christian Century, November 11, 2000.

Chapter 15: Treasure
[1]Winnie Varghese, "The Price of Compromise," Episcopal Life, October 1, 2006: 19, http://www.episcopalchurch.org/26769_78160_ENG_HTM.htm (accessed January 2008)

[2]Wuthnow, 131.

[3]Ibid., 52.

BIBLIOGRAPHY

Alkire, Sabine and Edmund Newell. What Can One Person Do? Faith to Heal a Broken World. New York: Church Publishing, 2005.

Armentrout, Donald. An Episcopal Dictionary of the Church. New York: Church Publishing, 2000.

Bernardin, Joseph. Introduction to the Episcopal Church. Harrisburg, PA: Morehouse Publishing, 1990.

Borsch, Frederick. The Spirit Searches Everything: Keeping Life's Questions. Cambridge, MA: Cowley, 2005.

Buechner, Frederick. Listening to Your Life. New York: HarperOne, 1992.

Butler Bass, Diana. Christianity for the Rest of Us: How the Neighborhood Church is Transforming the Faith. San Francisco: Harper, 2006.

Countryman, L. William. Forgiven and Forgiving. Harrisburg, PA: Morehouse Publishing, 1998.

Danforth, John. Faith and Politics: How the Moral Values Debate Divides America and How to Move Forward Together. New York: Viking, 2006.

Dawn, Marva. Reaching Out Without Dumbing Down: A Theology of Worship for this Urgent Time. Grand Rapids: Eerdmans, 1995.

de Zengotita, Thomas. Mediated: How the Media Shapes Your World and the Way You Live In It. (New York: Bloomsbury, 2005)

Fenhagen, James C. The Anglican Way. (Cincinnati: Forward Movement, 1981)

Ferlo, Roger. Opening the Bible, (The New Church's Teaching Series, v. 2). (Boston: Cowley, 1997)

Giles, Richard. Always Open: Being an Anglican Today. (Cambridge, MA: Cowley, 2005)

Hein, David and Gardiner H. Shattuck, Jr. The Episcopalians. (New York: Church Publishing, 2004)

Kinnaman, David and Gabe Lyons. UnChristian: What a New Generation Really Thinks About Christianity. (Grand Rapids: Baker, 2007)

Krumm, John. Why Choose the Episcopal Church?. (Cincinnati: Forward Movement, 1974)

Latourette, Kenneth Scott. A History of Christianity, Vol. 1. (Harper: San Francisco, 1975)

Lee, Jeffrey. Opening the Prayer Book, (The New Church's Teaching Series, v. 7). (Boston: Cowley, 1999)

Maynard, Dennis. Those Episkopols. (La Jolla, CA: Dionysus Publications, 1994)

Mitchell, Leonel L. Praying Shapes Believing: A Theological Commentary on the Book of Common Prayer. (Harrisburg, PA: Morehouse Publishing, 1985)

Moorman, John R. H. A History of the Church in England. (London: Adam and Charles Black, 1976)

Peacocke, Arthur. Paths from Science Towards God. (Oxford: Oneworld Publications, 2001)

Polkinghorne, John. The God of Hope and the End of the World. (New Haven: Yale University Press, 2002)

Polkinghorne, John. Quarks, Chaos and Christianity: Questions to Science and Religion. (New York: Crossroad, 1996)

Roof, Wade Clark. Spiritual Marketplace: Baby Boomers and the Remaking of American Religion. (Princeton: Princeton University Press, 1999)

Sachs, Jeffrey D. The End of Poverty: Economic Possibilities for Our Time. (New York: Penguin Press, 2005)

Sider, Ron. Rich Christians in An Age of Poverty: Moving from Affluence to Generosity. (Nashville: Thomas Nelson Publisher, 1997)

Smith, George Wayne. Admirable Simplicity: Principles for Worship Planning in the Episcopal Tradition. (New York: Church Publishing, 2001)

Snydor, William. Looking at the Episcopal Church. (Harrisburg, PA: Morehouse, 1996)

Tucker, Beverly D. and William H. Swantos, Jr. Questions on the Way: A Catechism Based on the Book of Common Prayer. (Cincinnati: Forward Movement, 2006)

Webber, Christopher and Frank Griswold III. Welcome to the Episcopal Church! (1999, Morehouse Group).

Weir, Allison. Henry VIII: King and Court. (London: Pimlico, 2002)

Wuthnow, Robert. All in Sync. (University of California Press: Berkeley and Los Angeles, CA, 2003)

WEB RESOURCES

www.kiva.org
> Help someone work their way out of poverty

www.globalrichlist.com
> How rich are you vs. the rest of the world?

www.e4gr.org
> Episcopalians for Global Reconciliation

www.nothingbutnets.org
> Buy a mosquito net, save a life

www.er-d.org
> See how the Episcopal Church helps heal the world

www.explorefaith.org
Learn more about religion
www.beliefnet.org
Learn even more about religion
www.LeaderResources.org
Find great curriculums. etc.
www.forwardmovement.org
Find great devotionals and other books
www.theforgivenessproject.com
Amazing stories of forgiveness
www.cred.tv
Fair trade jewelry
www.episcopalchurch.org/elife and www.episcopalcafe.org
Get connected with the Episcopal Church
www.episcopalchurch.org/peace_justice.htm
Episcopal Church's Office of Peace and Justice
www.er-d.org/eppn.htm
Lobby for justice
www.eenonline.org
The Episcopal Ecological Network
www.franciscan-anglican.com/enaw
Episcopal Network for Animals
www.freerice.com
Feed the world while building your vocabulary
www.episcopalchurch.org
Official website of the Episcopal Church
www.theredbook.org
Find an Episcopal parish near you
http://andromeda.rutgers.edu/~lcrew/
Fun collection of facts, charts and statistics about the Episcopal Church
www.sarahlaughed.net
A helpful lectionary blog
www.dayone.org
Download relevant sermon podcasts from brilliant preachers
from a variety of Christian ministers
www.cathedral.org/cathedral
Download podcasts from Washington National Cathedral
www.LeaderResources.org/Jesuswasanepiscopalian
Find even more resources and contact the author

Made in the USA
Lexington, KY
26 July 2013